1851-1951

MASSACHUSETTS MUTUAL

A GREAT NAME IN LIFE INSURANCE

FOR ONE HUNDRED YEARS

A CENTURY OF SERVICE

The Massachusetts Mutual Story

Doorway to Security

A Century of Service

The Massachusetts Mutual Story

by RICHARD HOOKER

Illustrations by R. J. HOLDEN

MASSACHUSETTS MUTUAL LIFE INSURANCE COMPANY

SPRINGFIELD, MASSACHUSETTS

To those who founded the

MASSACHUSETTS MUTUAL LIFE INSURANCE COMPANY

and to those who through the years have been responsible

for its sound operation and substantial growth,

this book is dedicated.

Foreword

THIS HISTORY of the Massachusetts Mutual has been a pleasant task. When President Alexander T. Maclean, whose untimely death occurred during its preparation, asked me to write it, in anticipation of the Company's centennial, he emphasized that the invitation carried with it complete freedom of expression. That condition has generously been kept implicit as the work has progressed.

It would, however, be both unappreciative and presumptuous on my part if I permitted the reader to assume that I had personally arrived at so complete a command of the mathematical and other intricacies of life insurance as the text might indicate. On the contrary, I have not only had, at all times, the fullest co-operation of the Company's officers in approaching such problems as that of an equitable application of the principle of non-forfeiture on lapsed policies, but in a number of instances the officers, especially President Leland J. Kalmbach himself, have provided carefully written expository statements which have been directly incorporated in the text. A complete list of those who have furnished such statements, more general memoranda, or invaluable verbal interpretations of different phases of the Company's business, would be impossible. But my special thanks are due to Vice President Harry H. Peirce and to Actuary Louis Levinson for comments and suggestions on many matters. Most of all, however, my thanks are due to James M. Blake, manager of field service, who has acted not merely as liaison officer in furnishing the material sought in countless queries but as guide, counsellor and friend in the whole undertaking.

The task has been made easier by the articles, notes and other memorabilia in regard to the Massachusetts Mutual's history which had been assembled by the late Winthrop S. Bagg, who in his final years of service to the Company devoted himself especially to preserving such material. Much vital information has also been obtained from the admirable thesis, "A History of the Clauses of the Massachusetts Mutual Contracts," which Miss Lillian E. Modig (now Mrs. Donald E. Pike and retired from the Company's employ) submitted to the Life Office Management Association.

Outside of the Company's Home Office, grateful acknowledgment is due to the friendly service of Springfield's most trustworthy historian, the late Harry A. Wright, author and editor of "The Story of Western Massachusetts" who, before his death in October, 1950, had given aid in establishing the local background; and to Miss Alice K. Moore, librarian of the Springfield City Library's historical collection in the Connecticut Valley Historical Museum, for important material of many kinds, both pictures and facts.

The quotations from "Elizur Wright; The Father of Life Insurance," by P. G. Wright and E. Q. Wright, have been made with the permission of the publisher, The University of Chicago Press. It should be added that Mr. Holden's imaginative drawing, "Elizur Wright before the Massachusetts Legislature pleading for the protection of policyholders," which serves as a headpiece to Chapter III, is not a representation of any single, recorded episode. It symbolizes the siege which, through the years, was conducted by Elizur Wright, with the result that Massachusetts was eventually placed in the acknowledged forefront of all the states with regard to life insurance legislation.

RICHARD HOOKER.

TABLE OF CONTENTS

Main Street, Springfield, with Western Railroad Station, built in 1851, and once famous Massasoit House.

CHAPTER I

The Founding

To TURN BACK the hands of the clock for the hundred years that have passed since the Massachusetts Mutual Life Insurance Company was founded in 1851 is a fascinating adventure. The single room, unheated save by a feeble stove, in the old Foot Block in Springfield, where the Company's second Home Office building is to rise nearly sixty years later, becomes the center around which a strange but active and rapidly changing world constructs itself. No wires go out from that bare office. It has but one table, two desks, three chairs, an earlier map of Springfield and pictures of George Washington and Abraham Lincoln— uncanny foresight on someone's part, for not quite yet

1

does Lincoln loom large on the national horizon. But, spread on the Company's records are the varied evidences, terse in themselves yet picturesque and colorful in what they suggest, of life as it was in this country at the middle of the last century.

Down in Washington, Millard Fillmore of New York is in the White House. Last year, as part of the Compromise of 1850, he signed the Fugitive Slave Act. That spells trouble. Earlier last year he moved up, as Vice Presidents do when Presidents die. Too much iced milk, and too many cherries eaten against his doctor's orders on a hot July day, caused a fatal rebellion in the innards of Zachary Taylor. "Old Rough and Ready" was elected President in 1848 as a hero of the Mexican War, which he had virtually ended in northern Mexico by his defeat of Santa Anna at Buena Vista in 1847. But the iced milk and the cherries did to the old soldier and frontier fighter what the Mexicans and the Indians could not. So Fillmore is now the Nation's head.

Here in Springfield, Main Street in front of the Massachusetts Mutual's office is unpaved. The sidewalks are of wood. At the corners, there are planks on which to cross the streets and escape the mud of spring and fall. Over those sidewalks pass women in hoop skirts and tight, encircling black satin bonnets, on the arms of escorts in stovepipe hats who may wear flowing capes, or even shawls like the one Lincoln will make historic. Hitching posts line those streets. It is the age of the horse. But not for nearly twenty years will horses, aided on certain steep hills by waiting mules, draw street cars in Springfield. Sanitation is such that to call it primitive is better than to describe it. The era of athletic sports which, like life insurance itself, is to contribute so much to make American civilization distinctive, has not

2

begun. The telephone and the typewriter are a quarter century away. The safety bicycle is a little further in the future and the automobile, moving pictures and the radio a half century or more. The amazing calculating machines on which business of many kinds, but especially life insurance with its multiple batteries of them, will one day depend, are undreamed of. Premiums must be figured and letters must be written in that one-room office by cramped but patient hands.

Yet the outer barricades of science, a growing knowledge of which through the coming century is to bring the marvels of the machine age and the threat of atomic war, have been penetrated. Steam is bringing railroads, steamships and more mills than New England water power alone can serve. Gas for lighting purposes has been known, even in a New England town like Springfield, for a few years. Over in Boston, Morton has demonstrated the mercies of anesthesia. Across the ocean, Charles Darwin is nearly ready to issue a challenge to new thinking on the origin of man. Morse's telegraph is working and, although an Atlantic cable has not yet been permanently laid, is bringing a new era in the exchange of what is called "magnetic news," some of it grim and foreboding, from all parts of the Nation. Life insurance itself is only an old idea given force by a new sense of what human co-operation can accomplish. But the boundaries of what men do and of what men try are being expanded, like the boundaries of their thoughts.

So the American scene in 1851, of which the Massachusetts Mutual promptly became a part, recreates itself one hundred years afterward.

Two years before, the California gold rush had begun. The ink was hardly dry on the Massachusetts Mutual's charter when its directors considered the question whether they would accept "California risks." Some phases of the lurid melodrama across the continent, which was to have its climax in "Champagne Days" in San Francisco, did not make those risks wholly appealing to a new insurance company. Its prudent officers wished for policyholders who, at a great age, would die peacefully in bed. They were less interested in men who might die earlier but more dramatically in their boots. Yet the new Company was in business to grow and to succeed. Even "California risks" had some attraction, provided the premiums paid were large enough. So it was decided that, on the basis of extra premiums, "California risks" should be taken.

The distance across the continent was then no measure of the real distance to California. Many of the gold seekers feared other dangers less than those of Indians on the plains and snows in the mountains. With no transcontinental railroad yet laid, they preferred, in advance, the route by the Isthmus of Panama. Its jungles and its fevers figure in the Massachusetts Mutual's records. The first of all the claims which the Company had to pay was on the life of Charles Desotell who was insured for $1,000 in January, 1852. He died on March 7, 1852, on a ship bound from Panama to San Francisco, his body being buried at sea. In his case, "California risks" had worked out too quickly for the Company. The Panama route had worked out badly for him. After experience, those who tried one route, whichever it was, seemed satisfied that the other must be better, if only because it could not be worse. But, by neither route was the distance so great as the difference between the wild excitement of San Francisco, the violence of the mining camps and the sprawling but prosperous old New England town

4

Foot's Block, corner of Main and State Streets, where the Company in 1851 begins business in its first, one-room office.

in which the new insurance company had been born. California was a vortex of whirling change. In comparison, New England represented a long established order. Yet New England had seen changes and was soon to see more.

Steam, recently added to the easily harnessed power of New England's rivers, was accomplishing the so-called industrial revolution. Factory workers were being drawn into fast growing centers. Unlike some other New England cities, Springfield today gives little visible evidence that water power had much to do with its founding or development. The power generated by Mill River seems relatively puny. But Mill River was actually an important factor, through obvious availability for a grist mill, in the location of the original settlement. Later its service to an iron forge shop influenced the location of the Springfield Armory and led

5

to the naming of Watershops Pond, on which one division of the Armory is situated and out of which Mill River flows. Washington himself shared in the early decision, overruling the Continental Congress, to make Springfield, and not Brookfield, more than thirty miles away, the site of the depot or arsenal which eventually was to become the Springfield Armory, manufacturing Springfield rifles, Garand rifles and machine guns. That decision had also been influenced by the fact that, while hostile British ships would be prevented by the Enfield Rapids from sailing up the Connecticut to Springfield, logs which might furnish gun stocks could easily be floated down to Springfield.

The vigorous determination and community spirit, which, in spite of unexpected obstacles, made the founding of the Massachusetts Mutual possible, had prevented Springfield, more than a decade before, from being isolated at the end of a spur track. It had made the railroads more important to her growth in a new era than the river had been in the old. In both episodes the community saw a challenge and met it. There had been danger that Springfield would be by-passed when the first rail routes were planned. But her leaders, later to be included among the founders of the Massachusetts Mutual, were ready not only to subscribe to railroad stock but to drive over rough country roads to Worcester, or wherever else, to establish Springfield's right to be the railroad hub of Western New England. They were sturdy defenders of their rights. Eastern Massachusetts was more populous, but, as time went on, the eastern leaders, in business as well as in politics, found it wise to consult and propitiate the "river gods," as they were known. The most influential of those gods came from Springfield. So first there were rails to Worcester and Boston on the east; then to

6

Albany and beyond on the west. Next to Hartford, New Haven and New York (although at first by steamboat from New Haven) on the south. Finally, to Greenfield and beyond on the north. These were the spokes which made the hub.

In spite of what steam had done for Springfield, those first directors of the Massachusetts Mutual had reservations about it. To them its advantages also spelled new dangers. They were properly anxious lest what seemed to be the high risk of one class of policyholders might impair the security offered to others. So on September 29, 1851, before the Massachusetts Mutual was six months old, or two months in active business, the directors voted that: "One quarter of 1 per cent on the amount insured be charged in addition to the regular rates of premium, for insurance on the lives of persons regularly employed on RailRoad Trains and Steamboats, as Engineers or Firemen in Steam Mills or Steam Factories, Express Carriers, or in Lake or river, or other inland navigation." Boilers would sometimes blow up, even at steam pressures which now seem so absurdly low as to suggest the toy engine of a child. One of the greatest marine disasters of all time came in 1865 when the boiler of the Mississippi river steamer *Sultana* exploded and 1,450 were killed.

One is reminded, by another entry in the minutes of the directors of the Massachusetts Mutual that in 1851 the whaling fleet, based on New Bedford, still put out on long and profitable voyages to distant seas. "Moby Dick," our great American classic, was published the year the Company was founded. It makes one think of Herman Melville, of the great white whale, and of Captain Ahab with his whalebone leg, to read that on November 4, 1851, the directors

7

voted: "That the application of William Pulsifer for insurance on the life of William A. Pulsifer, a common sailor, on a whaling expedition, be accepted and the extra rate of premium fixed by the secretary and general agent." So far as can be learned, young Mr. Pulsifer, assuming him to have been the son of the applicant, did not suffer the fate of Captain Ahab or the experience of Jonah. The directors therefore had no cause for permanent regret over their decision in this case. Yet they had their anxious moments, in those early years, at the thought of the death claims which any mail might bring. For there were times when there was little cash on hand or when money had actually been borrowed to pay the last claim that had been presented. There was a near panic in the office when Hiram Hitchcock of Chicopee, insured for $3,000 on November 10, 1852, died in May, 1853. The claim was not settled until August. Even then the money had to be borrowed. But the records show that there has been no other such delay in one hundred years.

The charter of the Massachusetts Mutual bears three names distinguished in Massachusetts history. George S. Boutwell signed it as governor on May 15, 1851, making that the effective date. It had been signed the day before by Henry Wilson, as president of the Senate, and on May 10th by Nathaniel P. Banks, as speaker of the House of Representatives. Boutwell was afterward Secretary of the Treasury in the Grant administration. As a respected elder statesman he lived until 1905, when he died at eighty-seven. Wilson, sometimes known as "the cobbler statesman" because of his humble start at a shoemaker's bench, was a noted anti-slaveryite. He later became a United States senator. When Grant was re-elected President in 1872 Wilson was elected

8

*The hazards of whaling add to the anxieties
of the Company's early directors.*

Vice President and died, while holding that office, in 1875.
As an anti-slavery leader and political figure Wilson was the
most prominent of the three. But Banks, by actual participation in the field, shared more directly than either of
the others in the conflict which ten years later turned into a
tragic resort to arms between North and South. By that
time Banks had become a member of Congress. He was one
politician who made good as a soldier. Advanced to the
rank of major general, he commanded the Union troops at
the capture of Port Hudson and received the formal thanks
of Congress for his leadership in that action. Such was the
aftermath of the national illusion of the time in which the
Massachusetts Mutual was born.

The illusion was that by the Compromise of 1850, offered
by Henry Clay and accepted by Daniel Webster, the slavery

9

issue had been settled. There were those in the North, and those in the South, who did not believe in the illusion or that the compromise would last. In the North they included Garrison and those who were called fanatical abolitionists. In the South they had been led by John C. Calhoun. The great South Carolinian, always of superb courage, had dragged himself into the Senate with his dying strength to hear Webster, both his foe and his friend, make the "Seventh of March" speech in 1850. Calhoun, in pure intellect the peer of either Clay or Webster, foresaw then, as with prophetic vision he had foreseen through many years, that Northern industrial capitalism would ultimately prevail. What he could not foresee was that one hundred years later there would be some reversal as Northern industries moved to Southern states.

Yet when Neville Chamberlain came back from Munich in 1938 with his umbrella he was hardly more confident of "peace in our time" than many of the citizens of places like Springfield were in 1851. Slavery as an issue had been exorcised from American politics—that, at least, was what they were told and told again in the editorial columns of their newspapers. The illusion of 1851 was not quite as ironically brief as that of 1938, but it faded soon. Yet the Compromise of 1850, on which the illusion was based, postponed the Civil War for ten years. During those ten years sentiment for the Union grew stronger. As for sentiment on the slavery question, late in the year the Massachusetts Mutual was born, Harriet Beecher Stowe's history-making "Uncle Tom's Cabin" began its serial magazine appearance in *The National Era* and was published in book form in 1852.

Aside from what became the irreconcilable conflict, it was not a time—perhaps there has never been one—when the community in which the Massachusetts Mutual was founded took its politics lightly and calmly. It was not, and it is not, a community of that kind. A month before the granting of the Company's charter had come Springfield's annual town election. It was close and it was heated. The Whigs denounced the "Locofocos," as they called the Democrats, and the Democrats denounced the Whigs. It was something of a drawn battle, but the Whig organ bitterly declared, in castigating the Whigs for not turning out in greater numbers, that it was not their fault that the "Locofocos" had not made a clean sweep of the whole town government instead of gaining something close to an even split. Apparently the Springfield Whigs were suffering from the creeping paralysis which caused their party soon to die and, in dying, to make way for the Republican party and to earn for itself the epitaph that it came to its end "through trying to swallow slavery." But the name "Locofocos," which the Whigs applied to the Democrats, is significant of the time. It came from a meeting of New York Democrats at which two rival factions sought control. One faction, or gang, turned off the then new gaslights. At that the other gang, who had come prepared, took the even newer friction matches, called "Locofocos," from their pockets, and made enough light for the meeting to proceed.

A few weeks before, Daniel Webster, "Black Daniel," looking old and unwell, had stopped overnight in Springfield. He was near the end of his great career, but still had the power that commanded men's loyalty, even when they thought him wrong, as in his "Seventh of March" speech the year before on the compromise on the slavery issue. Meanwhile out in that other Springfield in Illinois, "a bronzed, lank man," the circuit-riding "prairie lawyer" who was to

11

*George W. Rice, the leading spirit in the founding
of the Massachusetts Mutual.*

"forget himself into immortality" in his later service to the Nation, was telling stories in and out of courtrooms, while he studied men and books, but chiefly men and how to reach their minds and touch their hearts.

Such were the times in which Nathaniel P. Banks, Henry Wilson and George S. Boutwell, by adding their signatures to a piece of paper, cleared the way for the Massachusetts Mutual to begin.

Of more moment to this history than the state officials who signed the charter are the Springfield men who petitioned for it and those who, as its early officers and directors, steered the Massachusetts Mutual on a safe course in a dangerous period. It was a period when, within the recent past, many insurance companies had been organized. But it was also a period in which through ignorance, bad management or worse, they all too frequently came to grief and, in their failure, brought added hardship instead of more security to the families of those who insured in them. The moving spirit in the formation of Massachusetts Mutual was George W. Rice, a vigorous and alert man, barely in his thirties. As an agent in Springfield for the Connecticut Mutual of Hartford, he had not only seen written, but had himself written, much business that he thought might just as well be handled by a Springfield company. That was the community challenge.

It was George W. Rice's idea from the first that the new Company, as its name was to indicate, should be mutual and be wholly owned by its policyholders. He also assumed that this could be done in Massachusetts, as it had already been done elsewhere, without the need of an initial stock subscription. One of the advantages of our American system of government is that the separate states serve each other as legal laboratories in which experiments can be made and

13

observed. But it does not follow that these laboratories have the same equipment. That was what Mr. Rice discovered. It proved that, under Massachusetts laws, an initial stock subscription of $100,000 would be necessary, although the Company was eventually to be fully mutualized by the retirement of this stock.

One hundred thousand dollars was a big sum for a little community of about 12,000 inhabitants, not yet a city, in a day when the dollar not only bought more, but took far more hard work to earn than it does today. Something of the change in monetary values is indicated by the fact that in the Springfield area railroad laborers were then paid 72 cents a day. But Mr. Rice, who had the special support of Dr. Alfred Lambert, the Springfield physician who was his medical examiner for the Connecticut Mutual, was undaunted. He set to work and from thirty-one subscribers, none of whom pledged more than $5,000 individually, he finally secured the necessary $100,000. With that amount underwritten, the Massachusetts Legislature was successfully petitioned for the charter.

The original stock subscribers—their names and what they pledged will be found in the appendix—included most of the leading men in Springfield at that time. Otherwise it would not have been possible to raise the amount required in a community in which there were few men who could be called rich. Similarly, many of the subscribers were on the first board of directors. George W. Rice himself was not on the board, possibly because he continued for a time as the Springfield agent of the Connecticut Mutual. In spite of his youth he died a few years later and what might have been a career of high distinction in the history of life insurance was cut short.

14

*The modest furnishings of the first Home Office
match the Company's modest resources.*

Starting the Company was not easy even after the stock subscription had been nominally filled and the charter granted. At the directors' meeting on July 30, 1851, Colonel James M. Thompson resigned, both as vice president and director, because he was not satisfied with the security some of his fellow subscribers were putting up in support of their pledges. Colonel Thompson, one of Springfield's few rich men, undoubtedly had more means than some of the others and found it easier to put up gilt-edged security or cash whenever he went into a new venture.

The first president of the newly formed Company was Caleb Rice. He was also to become Springfield's first mayor a year later when it ceased to be a town and received its charter as a city. As president of the Massachusetts Mutual, Mr. Rice received a salary of $50 the first year and $100 the second year. Evidently his was not originally a full-time job. The employment of Francis B. Bacon as secretary, at the munificent salary of $800, indicated that, at first, as for some years afterward, the major labors were to fall on his patient shoulders. As a further evidence of the simple austerity of those times—"rugged" would be the current word for them—it is recorded that Mr. Bacon was obliged, in order to keep warm in winter in the Company's first one-room office, to sit with his "one good foot," the other apparently having been amputated, on the small stove. The office had been rented at $170 a year, but that cost was reduced by subletting desk space. Another indication of the Company's simple beginnings is found in the fact that the matter of purchasing a safe had to be considered at three directors' meetings before it was formally voted to buy one for $75. But the directors felt that a safe was necessary, since the president had a censurable habit of keeping too many valuable papers in his desk.

Caleb Rice, the first president of the Massachusetts Mutual, who guarded its destinies until 1873, although at first he did not perform such direct tasks as Francis B. Bacon, its secretary, was a man of unusual ability and quality. He was born in 1792 in Conway, Massachusetts, later to be the birthplace of Marshall Field, Chicago's "merchant prince." He graduated from Williams College in 1814. Afterward, as was the custom in those days, he read law in the office of William Blair, then prominent at the Massachusetts bar, in Westfield. In addition to being trained as a lawyer and having practiced for some years, Mr. Rice had served in the Legislature. But his most notable service had been as sheriff of Hampden County for twenty years, from 1831 to 1851. In that office his duty had been to arrange not life insurance, but an abrupt exit from this world, for any prisoners whom the

Caleb Rice, first president, 1851-1873.

courts ordered to be hanged. His election as Springfield's first mayor, after the granting of the municipal charter in 1852, further attests his standing. He was president of an early bank and the head of various public commissions.

It was sometimes claimed for Caleb Rice that he was Springfield's first citizen, when elected president of the new insurance company in his sixtieth year. But that honor actually belonged, if measured by historic prominence or by the breadth of his contemporary fame through the Nation, to another of the Massachusetts Mutual's original directors. This was George Ashmun, close friend of Daniel Webster, who had often come to Springfield to fish in Pecousic Brook, now part of Forest Park, with him. Ashmun had already attracted attention by able though brief service with Abraham Lincoln in Congress. His crowning distinction, however, was yet to come. In 1860 he served as chairman of the Republican national convention at Chicago which nominated Lincoln for President. He added to that service the following year, on the night Fort Sumter was fired upon, by prevailing upon Stephen A. Douglas, Lincoln's famous opponent, to announce to the country his loyal support of Lincoln.

There is no doubt that, for a long period, Ashmun was actually Springfield's first citizen and that he was the outstanding figure on the first board of directors of the Massachusetts Mutual. Yet he served as a director for but one year. There is reason to assume, and none to the contrary, that the decision not to serve longer was Ashmun's own. Although he had retired from Congress, he was often in Washington on legal business. Probably it was his inability regularly to attend the meetings of the board which led him to retire as a director. Nevertheless, his striking bril-

*Caleb Rice addresses a directors' meeting
in the first, one-room Home Office.*

liance, of which there is convincing evidence, serves, with
certain other characteristics, to emphasize by contrast the
less spectacular but solid qualities of his associates on the
first board of the Massachusetts Mutual—the men to whose
careful, prudent management the growth and success of the
Company were due. The fact was that, although Ashmun
might shine in the courtroom, in Congressional debate, or
at the Springfield dinner at which he amazed and delighted
William Makepeace Thackeray, the great English novelist,
he was not notably successful in the handling of his own
finances. He received large fees in famous cases but, as he
sadly admitted, the money was apt to be gone the next year.
When the Republican convention of 1860 approached, he
was short of funds. At first he did not plan to attend the
historic gathering over which he was destined to preside.

19

He decided to go to Chicago only when friends came to his aid with subscriptions amounting to $200.

Ashmun was a man of fine and sensitive honor. In a letter still in existence he expressed unwillingness to have his name pressed on Lincoln as a candidate for office. If every political supporter had the same reluctance to let his claims be advanced, the lot of each incoming President would be immeasurably eased. In countless cases we should have better Federal appointees. Ashmun's brilliance was thus coupled with fine scruples. But, because of the not always stable quality of that brilliance, his brief association with the Massachusetts Mutual emphasizes, by contrast, the different type of ability, the different type of leadership, which have made the Company what it is. One hundred years ago Springfield was only a town. Today, having been credited with a population of 162,600 by the census of 1950, Springfield is not a great city in size. But vigorous simplicity, strengthened by the standards of life in such a community, has contributed to and helped to shape the history which this book records.

Camp Banks, named after one of the signers of the Company's charter. Here Civil War soldiers trained.

CHAPTER II

Early Growth

IF TODAY it is an adventure to retrace the early history of the Massachusetts Mutual, it was, in a more realistic sense, an adventure, often an anxious one, for those who made that history. Perhaps their greatest asset, in addition to their determination, was their recognition that they were ignorant of what, to them, was very largely a new business. So they prudently set out to learn. In the minutes of one of the earliest meetings, June 3, 1851, before they had begun actual operation as an insurance company, is a record of a vote that "A. H. Avery and Harvey Danks be a committee to visit Boston and other places to collect information on the subject of insurance." What the Company accomplished in its early

21

Office of the Massachusetts Mutual Life Ins Co
Springfield Aug. 14 1851

Dear Sir

I send you herewith a pamphlet containing the organization, and system of business of the Massachusetts Mutual Life Ins. Co. which was incorporated at the last session of our Legislature. We have commenced operations this month, and are desirous of procuring a number of respectable and efficient agents in various parts of New England. Among others your name has been given as as a person likely to give satisfaction. It is our present plan to appoint agents who are not operating for other Life Insurance Companies. Our terms will be as liberal as other companies of a similar kind, and we will give such territory as an agent thinks he can thoroughly canvass. Will you please write, and inform me, if you think any thing can be done in your place in Life Insurance, and to what extent, also if you would give your personal attention to our interests should you be appointed as agent of our Co. Please answer at your earliest convenience

With much respect
Your
F. B. Bacon
Secretary

Copies sent to C.H. Bolles N Hampton
W.D. Sturtevant - Pittsfield
Cephas Crofts Lee
Geo F.S. Curtis Worcester
Clark Mills Rockville, Ct
J.F. Packard Monson

Secretary Bacon writes seeking agents for the Company.

years, and especially the pitfalls which it avoided, combine to suggest that Mr. Avery and Mr. Danks discovered, and then duly reported, much that was of value.

At the end of the first year, there were representatives at work in nearly every county in Massachusetts, and offices had been established in Boston; Providence, Rhode Island; Portland, Maine; and New Hampshire. These were soon followed by others at Vergennes, Vermont; and New Haven, Connecticut. The first annual report, in July, 1852, contained but six items. It reads as follows:

Received for premiums	-	-	- -	$11,532.22
Paid for expenses -	-	-	$3,716.96	
Commissions to agents	-	-	783.81	
Losses on 3 policies -	-	-	2,000.00	6,500.77
				$ 5,031.45

341 policies, $370,495 at risk.

The second annual report, in 1853, showed a few more items such as "surrenders," "advertising," "extra risks," "salaries," and "rent." It also showed total insurance in force of $547,895, represented by 422 policies, and "surplus on hand," $8,397. The fact that less business was written in the second year than the first appears to be explained by the fact that, when the Company began business, a considerable number of those who had subscribed to the original capital stock also took out policies in order further to aid the Company, as well as to establish security for their families. One of these, not unnaturally, had the distinction of being the first policy which the Company issued. Policy No. 1 for $1,200 was taken out by Harvey Danks, whose prominence among the founders of the Company has been indicated and who later became its Chicago agent. For some unexplained reason he eventually allowed it to lapse. Policies such as this, within what might be

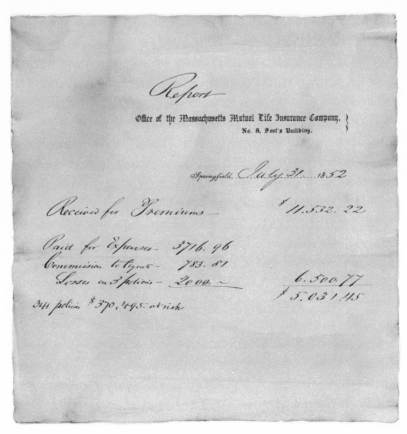

The first annual report.

called the Company's own family, were inevitably less numerous the second year. But from then on, progress was steady if at times slow. The Massachusetts Mutual soon achieved a comparatively strong position. Yet competition was keen with three other companies chartered in Massachusetts, while half a dozen more had representatives in the local field.

Hardly less significant than the figures indicating the Company's early growth were two votes taken by the directors.

On June 7, 1853, they met the question whether the Company's home offices should be moved to Boston. Apparently the matter had been held worthy of special consideration. But the answer was a ringing "No." Again on November 2, 1853, the question was faced whether the Massachusetts Mutual should permit itself to be merged with any other company. Again the answer was "No." The formal vote was that the directors "deem it inexpedient to entertain the proposition of uniting this Company with any other."

The Massachusetts Mutual, small though it then was, was in business to stay, and to stay in Springfield. This again reflects something of the community effort to meet a community challenge which the founding of the Company originally represented. But, at the same time, the directors were clear-headed enough to recognize that if the Company was to grow, Boston was the place in which the largest amount of business, as far as Massachusetts was concerned, must be found. That was stated before the directors as a fact with which they must deal. Provision was therefore made to give the Boston agency all the strength and resources that were possible.

When the Company began business, there was nothing to indicate what the mortality of lives insured in the United States would be. Actuaries, as we know them today, were rarely in the picture. Calculations combining the probabilities of life and death with compound interest had been, and continued to be, made by famous astronomers or professors of mathematics, such as Halley, Dr. Price, de Parcieux, De Morgan, and Gompertz.

Some time before the year 1844, Benjamin Peirce, Perkins Professor of Astronomy and Mathematics at Harvard University, had undertaken the preparation of a mortality table on

25

which to base premiums for life insurance issued by American companies. He studied most of the European mortality tables then known and finally, by what he called "a safe and judicious method," formed a special table by averaging for each age, from ten onward, the five highest chances of death shown by the Northampton, Carlisle, Equitable, Amicable, Swedish, Dutch and French tables. The first two were based upon "Bills of Mortality," or vital statistics recorded in the registers of certain parishes of the English towns named. The next two were drawn from the experience of pioneer English life insurance companies. The last three were constructed from parish registers, death rates among annuitants, and the lists of nominees in the French tontines, respectively. Of the French tontines there will be more to say.

The premium rates derived from Professor Peirce's table were available when the Massachusetts Mutual began business and were used by it for many years. It is remarkable that these premiums differed very slightly from those which would have been quoted had the experience of seventeen leading British insurance companies, later published as the "Actuaries Table" or "Combined Experience Table of Mortality," been then available for use in this country. Elizur Wright, the famous insurance commissioner of Massachusetts, decided as early as 1858 that the "Actuaries Table" was the most suitable standard he could find. He used it, with interest at the rate of 4 per cent per annum, to compute the life insurance liabilities of companies operating in the state.

The Company's very early growth was largely confined to New England. But it was not long before its operations expanded and the process began by which the Massachusetts Mutual eventually became a national institution with policyholders and investments in every state in the Union. The

Harvey Danks, first policyholder and first general agent.

year 1855 was especially notable. In that year offices were opened in New York, Albany, Cleveland, Chicago and Detroit and Harvey Danks, holder of the first policy, was established as the Company's superintendent in Chicago. By 1868, on the opening of an agency in San Francisco, the Company could be said to have spanned the continent.

A year before the founding of the Company the census of 1850 had set the population of the United States at 23,191,876. A century was to see that figure multiplied nearly sevenfold. As part of the multiplication, the year 1850 also saw 369,980 new immigrants landing on our shores. But against the tide of increase, both from births and from immigration, there were opposing factors. Infant mortality, by present-day standards, was appalling. Restrictions in early Massachusetts Mutual policies on travel and residence in the southern states, with special reference to coastal cities, were significant factors. Such restrictions become understandable when one finds that in 1853, the second year after the founding of the Company, an epidemic of yellow fever took 7,970 lives in New Orleans alone. That is a reminder to a more fortunate generation, to which yellow fever is unknown, that the docking of each new ship, in a time when health regulations were limited by the meager knowledge on which they were based, was a potential menace.

On December 4, 1860, the directors of the Massachusetts Mutual voted to subscribe "the sum of $50" toward a testimonial to Captain Wilson "of the schooner *Minnie Schiffer.*" The minutes yield no hint why the directors, who rejected other appeals, approved this one. But marine histories show that the passengers and crew—more than 400 in all—of the brand new steamer *Connaught* of the Galway line, making only her third voyage, owed their lives to Captain Wilson.

28

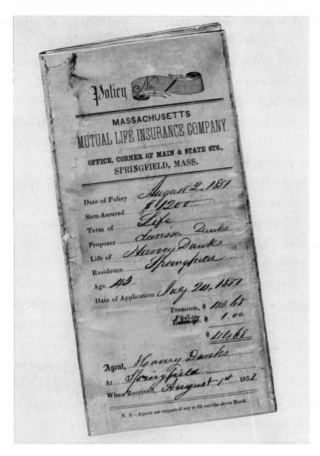

The Company's first policy.

Today such a dramatic episode at sea would command streamer headlines and extra editions long before the survivors reached shore. Actually the *Minnie Schiffer* was not a schooner but a tiny American brig of less than 200 tons. The tragic *Connaught* had caught fire and was burning helplessly when Captain Wilson steered the *Minnie Schiffer* close enough to rescue all aboard. He prevented the probable com-

29

pletion of one more of the many disasters of that early period of steam navigation which were listed under the grim heading "put to sea and never heard from."

But then there came the problem of bringing those 400 human beings, whose weight alone was a menace in the desperately overcrowded little American brig, safe to land before they starved or died of thirst. In this Captain Wilson succeeded. He was the hero of the hour, although those were days before such heroes were paraded up Broadway and showered with ticker tape. It seems possible that in the history of the seven seas so many had never before been saved by so few or by so small a vessel as the *Minnie Schiffer*. Whether or not there were any Massachusetts Mutual policyholders aboard the burned *Connaught* does not appear. But one suspects there were. Anyway the directors thought that $50 was not too much to contribute out of the Company's still meager and carefully guarded funds.

As the Massachusetts Mutual approached the end of its first decade, its business had grown to substantial proportions, thanks to prudent management which combined conservatism with progress. On January 1, 1861, the Company's assets were $381,743, its liabilities $327,054 and its insurance in force had risen to $5,628,980.

When Fort Sumter was fired upon and the long struggle between North and South took on a new and sterner form, as Lincoln issued his first call for volunteers, the Massachusetts Mutual was faced with the question of determining its position toward those who incurred the added risks of military service. The numerous occasions on which the matter was brought before the directors and the records of their various votes offer proof, if any is needed, that they approached the problem with a twofold anxiety and desire. They were anxious that the Company perform to the full its patriotic duty. But they recognized, as clearly as when they had considered "California risks" in the Company's very infancy, that they could not equitably assume the burden of "war risks" at inadequate premium rates without threatening the whole financial structure of the Company. It is not to be wondered at that one finds "war risks" mentioned again and again in the minutes of the directors' meetings as they considered and reconsidered a problem that was at once both new and grave. One is tempted, as one reads the records, to recreate in imagination not merely the physical scene, as those directors of nearly ninety years ago met to discharge their duties, but also to sense the spiritual atmosphere in which, with the burden on their souls of the news of Bull Run, Fredericksburg and Chancellorsville, they decided as wisely as they could.

Even for a later generation, which has seen and shared in two world wars, it is difficult to recapture the tension and sadness of those days. Failure followed failure and defeat followed defeat for the Union forces. The losses, both in battle and from camp diseases which medical science was then unable to control, mounted to relative proportions which a far greater population has not since known. Forty years after that struggle had ended, and a reunited Nation had turned to the tasks of peace, a story was still told by older Springfield residents whose memories stretched back to the Civil War.

In the darkest days one of Springfield's war mayors had called a mass meeting in the old, but then new, city hall to strengthen local support for the war effort. "Fellow citizens, ladies and gentlemen" began the worthy mayor in his unusual introductory address, "we are met to devise ways and means of ending this ———— ———— war and the Rev. Dr.

31

WAR PERMIT.

Extra Premium.

$100

POLICY NO. *943*

OFFICE OF MASSACHUSETTS MUTUAL LIFE INSURANCE COMPANY,

Springfield, *May 7th* 1862

In consideration of *Forty* Dollars paid in Cash, and a conditional note of *Sixty* Dollars, payable in twelve months from date, with interest, being *5* per cent Extra Premium charged on annexed Policy No. *943* the within named *John D. Fairbanks* is hereby permitted to enter the military service of the United States for the term of one year from the date hereof, *Provided*, such service shall not in any case be South of the thirty-fourth degree N. Latitude.

F. B. Bacon SECRETARY.

WAR PERMIT.

Extra Premium.

$100

POLICY NO. *2952*

OFFICE OF MASSACHUSETTS MUTUAL LIFE INSURANCE COMPANY,

Springfield, *Sept 17* 1862

In consideration of *One Hundred* Dollars paid in Cash, being *10* per cent Extra Premium charged on annexed Policy No. *2952* the within named *F. P. Brown* is hereby permitted to enter the military or naval service of the United States for the term of one year from the date hereof.

Without restriction as to locality at any season of the year

F. B. Bacon SECRETARY.

Typical Civil War permits, with and without geographical limitations, for policyholders entering military service.

Buckingham will now lead us in prayer." Thereupon the saintly Rev. Dr. Samuel G. Buckingham, whose long and beneficent pastorate at South Church was itself a chapter of Springfield history, rose from his seat and advanced to the front of the platform. Possibly he was sustained by the thought that in such a war such use of the Deity's name was not profanity in the ordinary sense and had in it some ele-

32

ment of righteousness. For, without a quaver, he besought divine aid and guidance in more conventional phrases. From that episode one gains an added sense of the spirit in which the directors of the Massachusetts Mutual gave their earnest thought to the problem of war risks, in a day long before the assumption of such risks by the Federal Government had been conceived of or "War Risk Insurance" had been born.

It was not far from the Massachusetts Mutual office that local training of troops for the Union armies was carried on. Less than a mile way, on what, as Hampden Park, was later famous in the world of horse-racing, bicycle-racing and college football, many recruits began life in army tents, shouldered Springfield rifles and went through their drill. Another camp was located between upper State Street and the railroad, and therefore nearer the present Home Office building. It was named Camp Banks after Nathaniel P. Banks who, as speaker of the lower house of the Massachusetts Legislature, had signed his name, ten years before, to the Massachusetts Mutual's charter. A third camp, known as Camp Reed, was also comparatively near the site of the present Home Office building, being located off Wilbraham Road.

In the minutes of the directors' meeting of November 4, 1862, appears this significant record: "The proofs of death of Israel Adams, policy 5733, which were laid on the table at the August meeting, were taken up, read and accepted, provided the secretary shall upon further inquiry be satisfied that the insured party was killed in a battle near the city of Richmond as alleged in the proofs and that the treasurer be authorized to pay the sum insured." The phrase "in battle near Richmond" raises the question "How near?"

September 9, 1867, saw the Company reach a long hoped-

*By 1866 the Company's growth requires erection
of this first Home Office building.*

for milestone in its history. On that day the stockholders voted, on recommendation of the directors, to carry out the intent of the founders. This was to make the Company mutual in fact as well as in name by retiring its capital stock and by establishing its policyholders as its owners. Thus, in a little over sixteen years from the signing of its first policy, prudent management and careful underwriting had established a surplus sufficient to justify the directors in passing this vote with regard to the capital stock of $100,000 which the laws of Massachusetts had made necessary. Three per cent had been paid on the stock in 1856, and 7 per cent annually thereafter.

It is an interesting historical coincidence that on the same day the directors voted to mutualize the Company they also felt justified, as the Nation recovered after the Civil War, in referring to the president, secretary and medical examiner, with authority to act, the matter of once more "issuing Southern risks." Their intent was to "insure" such risks, but the formal language of their action was to "issue." This was their recognition that not only was the Company to be mutual in fact as well as name, but that, also in fact as well as name, the reunion of the states into one Nation had been accomplished after four years of fratricidal strife.

At the annual meeting of the policyholders of the Massachusetts Mutual on January 26, 1870, a resolution was adopted, for presentation to the board of directors at their next meeting, which took note of the fact that Francis B. Bacon "who has been secretary of this Company from its formation, is by reason of severe illness lying in a precarious condition and unable to attend to business." A long record of devoted service to the Company, maintained under a severe physical handicap, had come to an end. The purpose of the

35

resolution was to recommend to the directors, and give them the support of the policyholders, that Mr. Bacon be continued on the payroll at the rate of $1,000 a year.

At that period, the provision of pensions, which is now not only practiced by the Company itself but which forms an increasing part of the business it performs for other corporations, was relatively rare. From the $800 which had been paid to Mr. Bacon in the Company's first year, his salary had been gradually increased to $4,500 in 1868. Born in Boston he had come to Springfield when a young man and was for some time engaged in the dry goods business. Subsequently he was a clerk in the Springfield freight office of the Western Railroad, leaving that position for the secretaryship of the Massachusetts Mutual at its organization in 1851. He served as secretary until, in January, 1870, failing health compelled him to resign and Charles McLean Knox was elected as his successor. On July 30, 1871, Mr. Bacon died.

It has been impossible to discover as much about Mr. Bacon as might be wished, either in the records or memorabilia of the Company or in the material in the Connecticut Valley Historical Museum or in the Springfield press. But it is established that, in addition to the faithfulness and unwearying attention with which he carried on the Company's business, almost single-handed for a considerable period, he was a man of exceptional courtesy, who gave the Company's office an atmosphere of welcome. No detailed statement of his physical handicap has been discovered but it is recorded in the Company's memorabilia that he sat with his "one good foot" on the stove in the first office, which seems to indicate that his other foot was insensitive, because artificial, and that at some time he had suffered amputation. On his death it was printed in the *Springfield Republican* that he [Mr. Bacon] began at the Massachusetts Mutual with Caleb Rice, "and the two worked admirably together, the executive ability of one, in the office of president, being finely supplemented by the grace and clerical fitness of the other."

Within twelve years of its founding the need of larger quarters for the Company had become clearly evident. The offices in the old Foot Block, originally a single room, had become increasingly inadequate. But the task of constructing a building especially for the Company's use, and to be owned by it, was approached cautiously. On October 6, 1863, it was voted, on the motion of E. W. Bond, who was later to become the Company's second president, that "the Company erect a suitable building on the land owned by them on Main Street, commencing next year." At this meeting it was voted to give notice to the next Legislature that "the Massachusetts Mutual Life Insurance Company intend to apply for an alteration of their charter so as to enable them to hold real estate to an amount not exceeding $50,000," and a committee was appointed to procure a plan and to report upon "the style, size and material and cost" of the proposed building.

As a further preparation for the new building, also as a reminder today of the degree to which many cities are built over what once were open brooks and undrained swamps, it was voted on May 1, 1866, that "the building committee examine the matter of drainage on Market Street [between which and Main Street the new building was to stand] and take such action thereon as to effect the operation as practicable." By that time, however, the problem of Springfield's unpaved streets had begun to be solved. Main Street had been progressively so raised, by the earth and gravel piled upon it to overcome swamp or mudhole, as to rise above the abut-

In 1873 the first Home Office building is gutted by fire.

ting properties. This was awkward for Main Street merchants and must have created new and artificial drainage problems for them. But a municipal election had already been hotly fought and won over the proposition to prepare for macadamizing Springfield's streets by buying a trap rock ledge, across the Connecticut in Westfield, from which to bring the necessary material.

The new building was finally completed and occupied in 1867-68. It was built of brownstone and was originally of four stories. For some years it was more than adequate. In addition to the rental of the ground floor for store purposes, quarters were also rented on an upper floor to the Masons.

In the bold handwriting of John A. Hall, who was later to be the Company's secretary and then its president during a peculiarly constructive period in its history, there appears this entry, as a historical interpolation made long afterward in the directors' minute book: "On the night of February 5, 1873, the Company's building was burned, and the front building completely gutted. Temporary quarters were secured in the Express Block on Court Street next east of City Hall which were occupied by the Company until the reoccupation of the Company's new building which occurred December 10th of the same year."

That fire, which started about 11 p.m., was so menacing to Springfield's business section that help was summoned from both Hartford and Worcester. Next morning, after the fire was out but the building a wreck, the Massachusetts Mutual gratefully served breakfast to all the fire-fighters at Haynes Hotel across Main Street. The total loss proved to be $100,000. The tenants suffered severely, but the chief loss, partially covered by insurance, was on the building. Little more than the walls of the main structure remained. The

39

heavy stone cornice, on which President Rice seems to have insisted in modifying the architect's original plan for a mansard roof, added to the scene of destruction. The big stone blocks which formed it had come plunging down on the sidewalk as the fire ate its way. As the building was reconstructed, with a fifth story, this heavy stone cornice was omitted and a conventional mansard roof added, apparently more in accordance with the architect's original design.

Again on February 8, 1891, a fire originating in the fourth floor quarters of the Masonic bodies caused a total loss of $30,000. In this case there was little interruption to the business of the Company, but it was decided that the time had come when, both for its growing needs and its greater protection, all of the building above the ground floor should be devoted to its own uses. The building still stands more than eighty years after its original erection. Having passed through various ownerships, following its sale by the Massachusetts Mutual, it is now occupied by a women's apparel shop.

The meeting of the directors on March 4, 1873, was notable for the adoption of resolutions on the death of the Company's first president, Caleb Rice, who had died on March 1, 1873, and for the election of Ephraim Ward Bond as the Company's second president. In addition to their appreciation of Mr. Rice's services and character, the directors declared: "In these days of loose notions of executive responsibility and looser administration of public trust we point with pride and pleasure to his [Mr. Rice's] long life spent in official employment—to a life of untarnished probity, of unsoiled honor, never even clouded by the breath of suspicion." In this expression is to be read something of the history of those troubled times. Careful and prudent citizens, like the directors of Massachusetts Mutual, were gravely disturbed not alone by such financial adventures as those of Jay Gould and "Jim" Fisk in the stock market, but also by the disclosures of official corruption in Washington.

One of the most interesting of the definite phases of the Massachusetts Mutual's early development is concerned with the conditions under which life insurance was solicited in those days. It seems a masterpiece of understatement to find, in a discriminating study of the evolution of the policies offered by the Massachusetts Mutual, the following: "It is difficult in this day to picture the condition under which those connected with insurance labored during the early days of this Company's existence." So far as the agent was concerned he was then usually engaged in some other business— conducting a general store for example—and insurance was only a sideline. In consequence, solicitation was apt to be casual. Yet, even in those days of insurance pioneering, it could be very earnest and enterprising.

A striking example was furnished by an agent in the field who, by such energy, rose to be the Company's third president. He was Martin Van Buren Edgerly, who signed his first contract with the Company in 1860 and was appointed general agent for New Hampshire in 1861. Subsequently he took on Vermont and Northern New York. Early in his service he went to the village of Hillsboro Bridge, New Hampshire, to see whether he could interest anybody in life insurance. He arrived at 5:00 p.m. and established himself in the little hotel. As the villagers came in to gossip at the close of the day he buttonholed them one by one. As they yielded to his persuasion, he sent them upstairs where the medical examiner, Dr. Hatch, made his home. At midnight, Dr. Hatch went to bed, a tired man, having made seven examinations in addition to his regular practice. At 3:00 a.m., however, Colonel

41

Edgerly had him up again. At 7:30 a.m., when Colonel Edgerly left town, he had eight signed applications in his pocket.

In the Company's files is an extraordinary letter which suggests both the conditions and the problems which surrounded the early sale of life insurance policies. Its spelling and grammar are so grotesque that it might seem to be the over-elaborate work of a professional humorist. But the original is available as evidence.

I come in Dunston and Gustmans often, before and after. They kipet shoestore and costem shop and sold leather and findings. I just coments for myself shoemaking. I netit tools, leather and lots a dings, so when i came ther in July to buy som ding, i seen a little book hang on a wall, i ask Mr. Dunston are you agend of life Ins. Co. He said, Yes, he ask if i woult go in to it, i toll him i not no. I ask him how much $1,000 woult cost for Life, he ask how olt i was on my last burday, i said i was 31 years olt on October 18 and he never ask me any more i answeret every question he ask me. He looket and said $23.40. i said its good deal money, a costomar came in store and he went in store and i went home. When i got there again and talket about it, i said i try it. He go to Dr. fullerton he lived 1 squere farder down i lived ½ mile up street. i dit not go that day, when i came down stopet Dr. fullerton was very warm day. Dr. f said uper your vest, he lessent my chist. he locket up and said wat the metter in here, i said do not knew, he sayd someding wistles in here, he sayd you go home and set on your shoe bench and work your way on, i be up in your house a day or so. So he dit all was right, i ask cost he sayd $1.00.

The same letter also illustrates one of the obstacles, which, in those days, the insurance agent frequently faced. It was the feeling that life insurance in eliminating some of the consequences of death, so far as one's dependents were concerned, must therefore be contrary to the law of God. Quoting again from the letter:

next time i came ther and talket about it i sayd i have tell my wife about it, i dit as i sayd. She comments lementen about 3 days. i

42

dont want such money as that. If you die jung Bible [did she mean "Bible" or "people"?] will say i killed you for money and so i give it up.

It was necessary for insurance agents constantly to contend with this religious objection and to prove, also by quoting scripture, that insurance was not against Biblical teachings. The early literature of the Massachusetts Mutual was replete, like that of other companies, in its insistence upon the propriety, from a strictly religious angle, of preparing through life insurance for the future of one's family. This scriptural quotation was used many times: "But if any provide not for his own and specially for those of his own house, he hath denied the faith, and is worse than an infidel."

The year the Massachusetts Mutual reached its quarter-century milestone the Nation celebrated its centennial. While the Company's officers were checking assets, insurance in force and the other chief items of progress, crowds were pressing about the exhibits of the great exposition at Philadelphia. Grant was still President. Henry Wilson, who had signed the Company's charter twenty-five years before, had died, the previous year, while Vice President. It was a time, like all important anniversaries, when eyes were turned both to the past and to the future. The rails across the continent, which had been lacking in 1851 when the Massachusetts Mutual was founded, had been successfully laid, the last symbolic spike driven into a crosstie having been the famous spike of gold. It was also a time when men of the age of those who now play senior golf and veteran tennis were limited to other diversions. Wearing stiff hats, stiff collars and abundant beards they drove fast trotters hitched to light, high-wheeled wagons. But their life expectancy, according to the actuaries of the Massachusetts Mutual and other careful companies, was less than that of their golfing grandsons today.

But the Philadelphia exposition was to be remembered, as much as for anything, for the demonstration by a Boston professor, born in Scotland, of an apparatus designed for the transmission of speech by electricity—the telephone. It was to alter the conditions of life in America, and the business of life insurance like every other business, hardly less than they had already been altered by the railroads. It was also the year that Thomas A. Edison established a new laboratory at an unheard of place in New Jersey. Soon he was known as the "Wizard of Menlo Park." There, one invention after another, making possible such things as incandescent electric lamps and moving pictures, was born of his genius.

The position of the Massachusetts Mutual at that time made a striking contrast with its earlier history. The twenty-fifth annual report for the year ending December 31, 1876, (the fiscal year having been changed to conform to the calendar year) recorded that the assets had risen from $5,031, shown by the first annual report in 1852, to $6,421,777. The death claims of $2,000 which had been paid on three policies in the Company's first year, had risen to $338,507 paid in 1876. In addition, $245,640 had been disbursed from surplus in the form of dividends to policyholders. There had also been paid $38,297 in the form of matured endowments. Thus, aside from "surrendered and canceled policies," represented under "disbursements" as $226,251, the total payments and credits to the Company's policyholders and beneficiaries made within a single year had increased from $2,000 in 1851-52 to $622,444 in 1876. In the first year insurance amounting to $370,495 had been issued to 341 individuals, including the Company's loyal organizers who helped to get it started by becoming policyholders themselves. In 1876 the number of new policies issued had risen to 1302 and the amount of insurance which they represented had risen to $3,624,000. Premiums received in the first year had been $11,532. In the twenty-fifth year they had increased to $1,058,459, in addition to which the Company received $360,303 in rents and interest, making its total receipts $1,418,762.

The Company had under it a firm foundation. The Home Office force was small, still to be counted on one's fingers. But that specialization of tasks which, to a peculiar degree, is the basis of life insurance operations, had begun. At the outset, Francis B. Bacon not only had to be the Company's actuary, but also had to perform other office duties and functions because, aside from the originally somewhat nominal duties of Caleb Rice as president, Bacon had been literally the whole force. But, in 1856, growing pains had set in and the directors had taken the decisive step of adding a clerk at a salary of $125 for the first six months and, "if satisfactory," at $175 for the remainder of his first year. One suspects that specialization, so far as that clerk was concerned, began with a broom. If so, he gallantly passed it on when a second clerk was added two years later. But Bacon was still the only actuary the Company had. This continued until 1869, when J. Weir Mason, now more identified, after the passage of time, by the black skull cap worn over his white hair than by any other circumstance, became the first so-called professional to fill that position. But Mr. Mason's connection with the Massachusetts Mutual was comparatively brief. He left in 1872 to become actuary of the Penn Mutual Life Insurance Company of Philadelphia. His departure marked the beginning of one of the longest and most notable careers by which the service of the Massachusetts Mutual has been distinguished.

As Mr. Mason's successor a soft-spoken young man was

brought on from New York, who served the Company until his death more than forty years later. This was Oscar B. Ireland, who won recognition as one of the outstanding actuaries of the country, eventually becoming president of the Actuarial Society of America. In that long period he also became not only a director of the Company, but a conspicuous and affectionately regarded member both of the office staff and of the Springfield community. Behind his gentle and kindly exterior there were not only the qualities of mental precision which his position required, but other qualities which a stranger might not at first have suspected. He had a flair for amateur acting and filled important roles in the polite and discreet comedies given, to the applause of enthusiastic Springfield audiences, before the turn of the century. But the sense of humor which such roles required was not his limit, as his scrap-books, filled with miscellany of many kinds besides the news of the insurance world, still attest.

Because of that sense of humor, and in the absence of any mark of authorship, one suspects that Mr. Ireland himself may have conceived one of the shrewdest satires in the history of life insurance. Carefully pasted in one of his scrap-books is a series of letters to the *Springfield Republican* which lack any signature save that of "Samuel Sharkey"—obviously a pseudonym for some one who knew life insurance up and down, inside and out. Robert Benchley could have done no better. But the time element and the orderly progress of the story compel these earthy letters, nominally written from a mythical place called "Bourbonville, Ill.," but actually from a spot probably no further away than the office of the Massachusetts Mutual, to be deferred to a later chapter.

46

*Elizur Wright before the Massachusetts Legislature
pleading for the protection of policyholders.*

CHAPTER III

Protection for the Policyholder

THE CHARACTER of the men who founded the Massachusetts
Mutual gave assurance that they would not manipulate it,
at the cost of its policyholders, for their own profit. This was
not always true of other companies either in England or in
this country. But, in addition to character and honest purpose, more was needed. There had to be a command of the
science of vital statistics; a command also of the mathematics
of finance. In addition, there had to be the will to apply to
life insurance clearly understood and sound principles that
had been conceived in such study of both the life span and of
the mathematical problems which finance presents.

No history of life insurance in this country, least of all a

47

life insurance company chartered in Massachusetts, can omit reference to Elizur Wright. By and large, but with some debits as well as credits, he deserves the recognition commonly given him as the greatest life insurance reformer. An extraordinary combination of qualities, seldom found in one man, equipped him for that role. He was a reformer, by nature, and an expert mathematician, by training. One quality gave him the insistent impulse for the correction of loose practices. The other gave him a key to the calculations, based on life expectancy and the return from invested funds, upon which life insurance depends. His father was a pious Calvinist who had delighted in abstruse mathematical calculations, but who feared, at times, that indulgence in them, for the very reason that they so appealed to him, was sinful. The son delighted also in mathematical calculations. But to him they were never sinful. He saw in them the means of serving countless men and women through life insurance and of righting the wrongs which had crept into its practices.

Wright's career as a reformer was divided into two phases. The slavery issue first aroused his intense feeling. He became one of the leading anti-slaveryites. Later he became interested in life insurance. On a visit to England in 1844 his passionate indignation had been excited by a spectacle which he saw in London at the Royal Exchange. As vividly described in that excellent biography, "Elizur Wright; The Father of Life Insurance," by Philip G. Wright and Elizabeth Q. Wright, he witnessed, "at the sublime center of trade," as he bitterly described it, the sale of "old policies on very aged men." The "aged men" were exhibited like cattle at a country fair. But there was one tragic difference. The older and more decrepit they were, the more attractive they became.

The purchasers of these policies, who thus became by

48

assignment the beneficiaries under them, undertook to maintain the annual premiums, which the old men were incapable of continuing, until the old men died. There was thus created a double evil. In addition to the wholly inadequate sums paid for the policies, the purchasers at once had a pecuniary interest—a very tempting and dangerous interest as experience proved—in the early death rather than the prolonged life of the insured.

More was amiss, however, with British life insurance, at that time, than the sale of policies on the lives of aged men who could not maintain their premiums. The fact that of the 300 British companies, formed within twenty-five years, no less than 250 had failed, indicated unsoundness; the circumstances of failure had too often caused suspicion of less than honest intent. It was clear, however, that much of this misfortune had been due to a lack of the mathematical knowledge which was required for conducting the life insurance business on a sound basis. To Elizur Wright the situation revealed three needs. One was to develop a mathematical basis which would assure the soundness of companies basing their operations on it. The second was to obtain legislation in this country that would compel them to operate on such a basis. The third was to obtain legislation that would compel them to deal justly with their policyholders.

Following his return, Wright's career was shaped by his recognition of those three needs in the service of life insurance in this country. In accordance with the contract into which he entered with six life insurance companies, he first engaged to prepare net valuation tables for their use. These tables, when applied to all the policies in force in any company, showed the reserve required, according to the mortality table and the interest rate used, in order to meet the

49

*Elizur Wright, greatest of life insurance reformers
and Massachusetts insurance commissioner.*

promises made under the several policies. This monumental work, which first won for him the title "The Father of Life Insurance," was completed with the aid of his older children in a little over a year and became available in 1853. Although the Massachusetts Mutual, founded two years before, was not one of the six original subscribing companies or one of the four others each of which received one of the ten hand-written copies, the tables were afterward printed in book form and all insurance companies profited by them. That, however, was only the first step in Wright's campaign to put life insurance in this country on a sounder basis than he found it in England.

Wright's next step was to bring every company chartered in Massachusetts under efficient state supervision. This required it to make detailed reports showing that it was maintaining the necessary reserves, according to his calculations as applied to each separate policy, and was therefore protecting its solvency and its capacity for honest service to the public. Having drafted a bill for this purpose and seen its defeat in the Massachusetts Legislature in 1854, he haunted the State House for the next four years "lobbying for the widow and orphan." In the end, in spite of rebuffs and ridicule which had disturbed him very little, his efforts were crowned with measurable success. When, in 1858, the bill which he had drafted was passed, he was appointed as one of the state's two insurance commissioners by Governor Banks, who as speaker of the House had signed the charter of the Massachusetts Mutual in 1851. Wright, with his extraordinary equipment, might well have been the sole commissioner—the other commissioner hardly counted. "Because of his mathematical grasp of the subject and his fiery zeal for reform" as justly set down by his biographers, "the

51

great work of the commission, without any reflection on his associate, may be attributed to him."

From that time on, as insurance commissioner for Massachusetts, Wright carried on a campaign of vigorous regulation. His administration was, in fact, so vigorous that he earned the hostility of some companies. In 1867 they were successful, through political manipulation, in causing him to be dropped from office. But in the eight years of his service as commissioner he had set new standards. These not only made it an advantage for any company like the Massachusetts Mutual to be known to be under his direct administration, but also forced companies chartered in other states to conform to the Massachusetts standards of solvency as long as they did business in Massachusetts. He drove no less than fourteen companies out of the state.

By a strange coincidence the case described as the most trying test of Wright's official integrity was that of the American Mutual of New Haven. Benjamin Silliman, the famous scientist, under whom Wright had studied as an undergraduate at Yale, was the nominal president of this company. But the active manager was Benjamin Noyes, Silliman's son-in-law. When Wright found, again quoting from his outstanding biography, that the company was spending no less than 50 cents of every dollar in "expense," that its reserves were impaired, that "many of its public statements were absolutely false and that it assured everybody irrespective of health," he threw the company out of Massachusetts and "advised the American public to have nothing to do with it."

The need that existed both for a reformer like Wright and for a company that was to be conducted along the lines of the Massachusetts Mutual is emphasized by another coincidence. In the spring of 1851, as the bill giving the Massachusetts

52

Mutual its charter was going through the successive stages of enactment in the state Legislature on its way to Governor Boutwell's desk, the news of such steps was printed in small space and type in the Springfield newspapers. But, printed in larger space and type on the front pages of those newspapers, were the advertisements of numerous insurance companies. Both the number and the prominence of these advertisements are a reminder of the degree to which, during the previous decade, the formation of new life insurance companies had been the fashion. In 1850, forty-seven companies were in the field, including three English companies which had established American agencies. A majority of these were less than two years old. It is significant that, of the entire forty-seven, only twelve continued actively in business for any considerable period.

The most striking fact about these insurance advertisements, with their extravagant promises, in the Springfield newspaper of 1851 is that conspicuous among them was the advertisement of the American Mutual Life Insurance Company of New Haven. This was the company with which Elizur Wright was to deal so sternly a few years later. But there was still another coincidence. As part of the American Mutual's glittering inducements there were printed, in proof of its fancied soundness, the names of a "Local Board of Reference." They were names which carried weight in Springfield. One of them was Rev. Dr. Samuel S. Buckingham of South Church, who later was to open with prayer that famous Civil War mass meeting. Another was Ephraim W. Bond, soon to be one of the original directors of the Massachusetts Mutual and later its second president. Two others were also to be on the Massachusetts Mutual's first board. Evidently they had been taken in, first by the great fame of

53

Professor Silliman of Yale who had let his name be used by his son-in-law as president of the American Mutual; second, by the alluring prospectus of a business they did not yet know too much about. That they all retired from the American Mutual's "Board of Local Reference" before its eventual disappearance is to be presumed. Their later connection with the Massachusetts Mutual must have been an education, apart from the contribution of Elizur Wright, in what insurance companies could prudently do.

Wright was no less severe with the International of London. It meant nothing to Wright that that company had several august noblemen on its board of directors or that its actuary was a fellow of the Royal Astronomical Society. By the pragmatic test of events Wright was proved, when the International failed some ten years later, to have performed a further service to those who, but for his act in expelling it from Massachusetts, might have been numbered among its unfortunate policyholders.

Wright was especially concerned, after he had accomplished his reforms assuring the solvency of companies, with the protection of policyholders who, like the "aged men" he had seen in London, had lapsed their policies because they were unable to continue premium payments. The absence of surrender values on policies, discontinued after they had been in force over a sufficient time to develop values, meant the loss, in the ensuing lapse, of a very substantial part of the premiums which had been paid. While some companies voluntarily provided cash values in such instances, in many cases lapse resulted in the total forfeiture of any value accumulated under the policy. Lapses, accordingly, comprised a profitable type of transaction. Some companies attempted to induce lapses by setting traps in the form of intricate

54

technicalities, or even in starting rumors of their own insolvency in order to frighten policyholders into ceasing premium payments.

Wright very wisely saw that there was a way to destroy this evil and, with this as his goal, he succeeded in getting through the Massachusetts Legislature the most famous of all his reform measures. This was the non-forfeiture law preventing companies from appropriating the reserves which had accumulated on lapsed policies. This law of 1861, as it is known because it went into effect that year, provided that the life insurance company should use four-fifths of the reserve on a lapsed policy to insure the life of the former policyholder for the full amount of the policy for as long a period of time after the policy had lapsed as this sum was sufficient to provide. It did not accomplish all that he sought, for it did not require payment either in paid-up insurance or in cash. Twenty years later the law of 1880 provided for paid-up insurance.

While there can be no question that Wright's services were very great, certain qualifications of the position he took in the practical application of the principle of non-forfeiture have become necessary. There may be mistakes in applying a principle that is thoroughly sound and honest. Life insurance history, enacted into more recent regulatory laws, has shown where Wright was wrong. His assumption, in applying the principle of non-forfeiture, was that the reserve carried to assure the payment of death claims was necessarily the proper basis upon which to compute non-forfeiture benefits to the policyholder. The recent drastic reduction in interest rates has resulted in a situation which has emphasized the fallacy of this assumption. Because of the prospect of continuing reduced interest earnings, many companies have voluntarily "strengthened reserves;" that is, they have applied additional sums of money to the reserve account to forestall difficulties in accumulating reserves sufficient to mature all policy contracts, by reason of the diminished interest earnings. It seems obvious that equity does not require that a policyholder who discontinues premium payments should be entitled to these additional reserves which were not contributed by him. Recent amendments to insurance laws permit the strengthening of reserves within certain limits without requiring an increase in non-forfeiture values, thereby preventing injustice to policyholders who do not let their policies lapse, and furnishing such policyholders additional protection. However, legislative changes of this kind, as much as they modify Wright's original ideas, are in harmony with the basic principles expressed in his great laws. The whole matter of control of the institution of life insurance through laws of this kind has come to present one of the most interesting phases of life insurance history.

The officers of the Massachusetts Mutual, like those of some other companies, were not at first in entire sympathy with the non-forfeiture law of 1861. In his report in 1862 Wright said, after discussing the adequacy of the extended term rates: "We cannot but indulge the hope that this view of the mortuary experience of the nineteen companies doing business in this State . . . will considerably relieve the apprehension and the despondency with which at least three of our home companies have viewed the legislation of last year. If they could be fairly reconciled to it as prudent and safe as well as equitable, they would no doubt use it with great effect, both at home and abroad, to increase business. The advantage of policies which are legally secured against any forfeiture of their net value is too great to be thrown away for any slight apprehension. It might easily be made to attract business far more than sufficient to compensate for the loss of any profit that could accrue to residual members from the forfeiture of policies."

The Massachusetts Mutual was one of the "three home companies" which, according to Wright's characteristically pungent, but sometimes exaggerated, language viewed the non-forfeiture law with "apprehension and despondency." The occasion for the comment, so far as the Massachusetts Mutual was concerned, was an insertion in the declaration clause of the application under which the insured waived his right to the non-forfeiture provision. This was done on the evident assumption that the Company had a right, despite the law, to enter into any contract to which the individual applicant, on a full statement and clear understanding of its terms, chose to become a party.

Insofar as this was a disagreement between Wright and the Massachusetts Mutual the disagreement, at that time, was short-lived. The clause waiving the right of non-forfeiture actually remained in the Company's application form for only five months. By the time Wright came to prepare his report of 1862, the Massachusetts Mutual had not only directed the change but the change had gone into effect.

Many times in their annual reports the successive presidents of the Massachusetts Mutual paid their tributes to Elizur Wright. The passage of time served only to emphasize the soundness of his fundamental approach in applying the non-forfeiture principle. His stand, as he predicted, became of great value to insurance companies chartered in Massachusetts when they competed with companies chartered in other states.

The non-forfeiture provision, aside from the precise

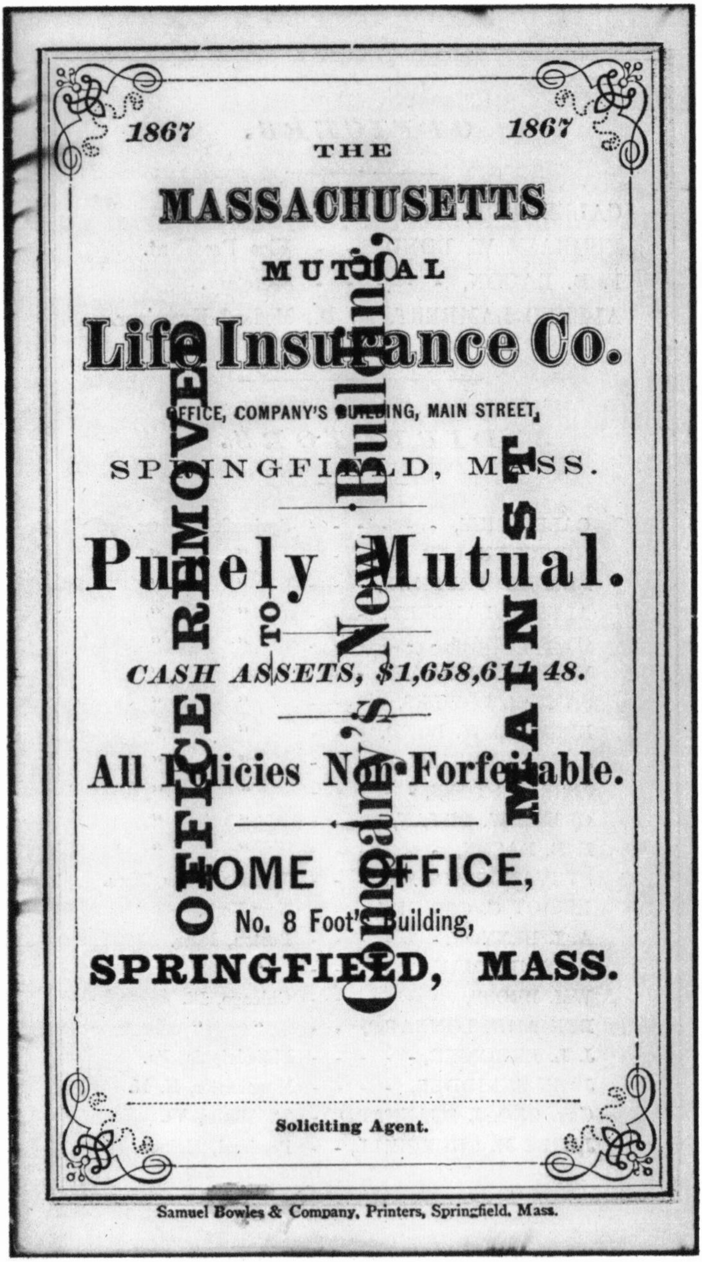

1867 1867

THE

MASSACHUSETTS

MUTUAL

Life Insurance Co.

OFFICE, COMPANY'S BUILDING, MAIN STREET,

SPRINGFIELD, MASS.

Purely Mutual.

CASH ASSETS, $1,658,611 48.

All Policies Non-Forfeitable.

HOME OFFICE,

No. 8 Foot's Building,

SPRINGFIELD, MASS.

OFFICE REMOVED TO Company's New Building, MAIN ST.

Soliciting Agent.

Samuel Bowles & Company, Printers, Springfield, Mass.

Title page from an 1867 Company folder.

DIFFERENT

Plans of Insurance.

THE MASSACHUSETTS
Mutual Life Insurance Co.

Issue Policies in all the most popular forms of Insurance.

ALL POLICIES NON-FORFEITABLE.

1. Life Policies—On which the Premium is to be paid annually during the continuance of life. See Table No. 1 A.

2. Ten Premium Life Policies—On which the whole Premium for life can be paid in ten annual payments ; the assured having the privilege, after the payment of at least two annual Premiums in Cash, provided application is made for that purpose before or within thirty days after the lapse of the Policy, of having the Policy converted into a paid up Policy, for as many tenths of the original sum insured, as annual *Cash Premiums* have been paid. See Table No. 1 B.

3. Twenty Premium Life Policies—On which the whole Premium for life can be paid in twenty annual payments, and after the payment of two annual Premiums in Cash, the assured can have the privilege of discontinuing further payments, and having the Policy converted into a paid up Policy for as many twentieths of the original sum insured as Annual Cash Premiums have been paid. See Table No. 1 C.

4. Single Premium Life Policies—Where the whole Premium for life can be made by a single payment, and the Policy becomes a source of income to the assured during life. See Table No. 1 D.

5. Endowment Policies—Payable to the assured upon arriving at a specified age, or to his representatives upon prior decease—Annual Premiums payable until the Policy becomes a claim. See Table No. 2.

6. Ten Payment Endowment Policies—On which ten Annual Premiums are to be paid, and payable at a specified age, or upon prior decease. See Table No. 3.

PREMIUMS may be paid in Cash, or if desired (when the Premium amounts to $40 and upward) Notes will be taken for one-third the amount of the Annual Premium, the interest on the Notes to be paid annually.

*Another page from the 1867 folder setting forth
"Different Plans of Insurance."*

59

formula by which it was figured, was of vital importance to the policyholder. Yet it was only one item in the early evolution of the policyholder's contract with the Massachusetts Mutual. That evolution is another index of contemporary history. As time went on many of the early limitations or restrictions were done away with. Experience showed either that their elimination was just or that their retention was unnecessary.

On October 3, 1871, the directors of the Massachusetts Mutual adopted, as on numerous occasions both before and after when conditions seemed to demand it, a new form of policy. This one was notable for the care with which it redefined and added to the limitations which had already been in force. The following clauses have today a historical interest which makes them worth quoting in the exact form in which they were adopted eighty years ago:

Sixth,—That in case the said person, whose life is hereby insured, shall be employed in mining, subterranean, or sub-marine occupations, or in the manufacture or transportation of gun-powder, nitro-glycerine, or other highly explosive material, or in case the said person shall be employed upon a railroad train, or steamboat, or sailing vessel, or as engineer or fireman of a steam engine, or shall enter into any military or naval service, (the militia not in active service excepted), or shall enter upon an aerial voyage, this Policy shall be null and void, *unless the express permission* of the said Company in writing, signed by the President or Secretary, be given to such person to be engaged in such employment or occupation.

Seventh,—That in case the said person, whose life is hereby insured, shall, without the written consent of said Company, signed by the President or Secretary, pass beyond the limits of the United States, (except as herein provided,) or shall, without such consent, between the first day of June and the first day of November, in any year, pass or remain within that portion of the United States lying south of thirty-six (36) degrees north latitude, which is within one hundred miles of the coast of the Atlantic Ocean, or Gulf of Mexico, or which is within fifty miles of the Mississippi, or Red Rivers, except while

60

journeying, and for a period not to exceed fifteen days at any one time, this Policy shall be null and void, *Provided, However,* that the said person has liberty to go as passenger between Europe and any of the Atlantic or Gulf ports in the United States; also to travel and reside indefinitely in the Dominion of Canada, and in Europe not south of forty-two (42) degrees north latitude; also to go on any passage by water, in a steam or sailing vessel along the coasts of the Dominion of Canada, (not north of fifty (50) degrees north latitude,) and the United States, with liberty to touch at any of the ports on said coasts, and in Cuba, except that said person shall not, between the first day of June and the first day of November in any year, remain (at any one time) for a period exceeding fifteen days in any one port of the passages above specified, lying south of thirty-six (36) degrees north latitude.

Eighth,—That in case the said person whose life is hereby insured, shall become so far intemperate in the use of alcoholic stimulants, opium, or other narcotic, as to seriously impair the health, or induce delirium tremens, or directly, or indirectly cause the death of the said person; or in case the said person shall die by his or her own hand, or act, whether sane or insane, or in, or in consequence of, a duel; or by the hands of justice; or in, or in consequence of, violating any law of any Nation, State, Province, or Municipality, this Policy shall be null and void.

The provision that the policy would become void if the holder should "enter upon an aerial voyage" referred to balloon ascensions. Apparently, barnstorming balloonists, who gave exhibits at county fairs, had multiplied until the risks taken by their numerous passengers became sufficient to attract the attention of careful insurance men.

One of the most picturesque episodes in Springfield history had been the ascension of one of these barnstorming balloonists, a Frenchman by the name of Bertin. He and his balloon were the novel attraction of the annual fair of the Hampden County Agricultural Society in the early days of the Massachusetts Mutual's career. A bigger crowd then gathered in Springfield than ever before. There was standing

61

New England winters once had features they now lack.

room only on incoming trains. Undoubtedly, some of the Company's directors, perhaps all of them, saw Monsieur Bertin sail away into the skies, although the inadequacy of his gas supply defeated his advertised purpose of taking with him, as passengers, two local citizens. But, although that episode might have convinced the Company's directors and officers, then and there, of the hazards of an "aerial voyage," evidently it did not. Careful search proves, on the contrary, that in no Massachusetts Mutual policy issued prior to 1871 did the provision against an "aerial voyage" appear.

The original introduction of the risks of "aerial voyages" makes it appropriate to refer at this point, although out of the exact chronological order, to the Company's later handling of the insurance problems which the Wright brothers unwittingly created by their successful experiments more than thirty years later. Early in the history of flight by "heavier-than-air machines," to distinguish planes from balloons, occasional flights as fare-paying passengers on established air lines could be made without forfeiture or the payment to the Massachusetts Mutual of extra premiums by policyholders who were forced to make such flights in emergencies. But if they made a practice of frequent flying they had to pay extra to maintain their life insurance protection. It was on the pilots and other crew members that the burden of extra premiums fell most heavily. Their extra premiums were relatively large.

Today, the Massachusetts Mutual has eliminated extra premiums for ordinary passenger flights, and the extra premiums for pilots and other crew members have been reduced to little more than one-tenth of what they once were. Such insurance rates, since they are carefully figured, furnish a better index of contemporary progress in aviation than big headlines over reports of occasional airplane disasters.

Returning to the chronological order, as transportation by means more usual than balloons became gradually safer, and as public sanitation somewhat haltingly improved, reducing the danger of epidemic diseases such as yellow fever and cholera, restrictions on travel and residence in specified geographical areas were progressively lifted. But for a considerable period travel and residence in the South cost the insured from 1 to 5 per cent of the amount of the policy as an extra premium. It will have been noted, in the restrictive clauses which have been quoted, that the policy became void if the death of the insured occurred "in, or in consequence of, a duel." This, too, had a background of colorful history.

The provision in regard to dueling went out before some others. In the fifty years before the Massachusetts Mutual

63

was founded there had been many duels with fatal results. The two most famous were that in which Aaron Burr killed Alexander Hamilton and that in which Andrew Jackson, long before he became President, killed Charles Dickinson in a dispute over a proposed horse race that was never run. But, in the fifty years which followed the Company's founding, dueling in this country, except for the mining camps and other turbulent centers of the Far West, went out of fashion as it had in England, partly through the influence of Prince Albert, Queen Victoria's consort. One of the most famous killings of the later period was that of "Jim" Fisk, Jay Gould's unscrupulous associate. But that was a duel only in the sense that it was the outgrowth of what was figuratively called "a duel for the affections of a lady." So the clause in the Massachusetts Mutual's contract with regard to dueling disappeared because dueling disappeared.

One of the criticisms of life insurance in the early days was that too many companies contested death claims in the courts on mere technicalities. It was, therefore, another step forward when, in 1889, the Massachusetts Mutual adopted a clause making its policies incontestable, after they had been in force for two years, on any other grounds than those of violations of the military or naval service restriction, nonpayment of premium (in which case the non-forfeiture clause directed the adjustment) and intentional misstatement. The protection of the policyholder had gone a long way forward.

*Springfield's covered bridge across the Connecticut
served both transportation and romance.*

CHAPTER IV

The Career Man Appears

No SERVANT of the Massachusetts Mutual in its one hundred years has left a more definite impression of personal quality than Ephraim Ward Bond, its second president, who filled that office from 1873 to 1886. But there was an equally definite distinction between him and his successors which is part of insurance history in general and of the Massachusetts Mutual in particular.

When Mr. Bond died in 1891, having continued to serve as a director after his resignation as president five years before, he was referred to in a long and highly appreciative review of his life in the *Springfield Republican* as being a fine "type of the old-school lawyer and gentleman." Even

65

Ephraim W. Bond, second president, 1873-1886.

for that type he had an unusually rich culture. He was born at West Brookfield in 1821 and graduated from Amherst College at the head of his class in 1841. Fired for a time with ambitions of authorship, he pursued postgraduate studies at Yale in English literature. He then decided, however, upon the law. Entering Harvard Law School, from which he graduated in 1844, he had close associations there with Rutherford B. Hayes, afterward President of the United States, and others who rose to national fame as lawyers and judges. Conscientious and public-spirited, Mr. Bond soon became one of the pillars of Springfield, where he opened a law office in 1845. The only criticism of him seems to have been that he had a "habit of being late at all appointments." He was a selectman of the town in 1848 and 1850. When sent to the Legislature in 1852 he was instrumental in securing the city charter. He was one of the pioneers in the establishment of the Springfield City Library, served as its president, strongly advocated the plan to make it free and helped by his financial contribution to make that possible. No worthy community effort found him unresponsive.

Mr. Bond's connection with the Massachusetts Mutual came through his association with E. D. Beach, with whom he formed a law partnership in 1850. Mr. Beach had been one of the original promoters of the Massachusetts Mutual when it was organized in 1851. On his death in 1867 Mr. Bond followed him as vice president. When Caleb Rice died in 1873 and Mr. Bond succeeded him as president, Mr. Bond had behind him more than a quarter century of lucrative law practice, but only a few years of not too close association with the insurance business. In addition to his ability, he was painstaking and the soul of courtesy. No other choice for the leadership of the Massachusetts Mutual would, at that time, have been appropriate. He was cautious and conservative, as "a gentleman of the old school" should be. In the thirteen years of his presidency the assets of the Massachusetts Mutual grew, but somewhat slowly, from $4,509,936 to $8,108,754.

What now seems, in view of the present size of the Company, a naive comment on its growth was published in 1884, toward the end of Mr. Bond's service as president, in "King's Handbook of Springfield." After giving a brief account of the history of the Company up to that time, this useful work observed:

It will probably be a surprise to many, even to its neighbors, to know that the business of the Massachusetts Mutual at the Home Office gives constant employment to three officers and fifteen clerks, besides janitor, real-estate man, and the local agency force; while, in nearly all the Northern States it has a force of agents at work securing new business. But when it is remembered that accounts have to be kept with over 14,000 separate policies; that perhaps a tenth as many cease, and a sixth as many new ones are added, in a year; that some $7,000,000 are to be kept safely invested and accounted for; and that nineteen separate state departments have to be furnished with an elaborate annual statement of the company's affairs,—it will be seen that there is plenty of work for all.

With the election of Colonel Martin Van Buren Edgerly as president of the Massachusetts Mutual in 1886, a new type of insurance executive appeared on the scene and a new chapter of insurance history began. Instead of the lawyer drafted for insurance service, as in the case of Caleb Rice and then of E. W. Bond, Colonel Edgerly represented the advent in the Company's ranks of the "career man." That phrase has, of late years, figured more and more frequently in insurance circles and insurance literature.

The Massachusetts Mutual, like other insurance companies, has established carefully organized training courses

68

An early view of Springfield and the Connecticut River.

for the education and development of those who are admitted to its ranks. They are more fortunate than Colonel Edgerly for there were no training courses in his day. The essence of his success was that he had taken advantage of such opportunities as then offered to train himself. When, at fifty-three, he became president of the Massachusetts Mutual, he was not suddenly charged, at a mature age, with new responsibilities in a new field. He was a "career man" who had begun in the insurance business twenty-seven years before as a comparative youth. He might be said to have thought insurance and—with respect for his aggressiveness —to have fought for insurance, from that time.

Colonel Edgerly was born in Barnstead, N. H., in 1833 and entered the life insurance business in Pittsfield in that state in 1859. In 1863 he moved to Manchester, N. H. and was so successful in soliciting insurance that the scope of his services

69

to the Massachusetts Mutual steadily broadened. In 1882 he became a director, in 1884 second vice president, and in 1885 vice president of the Company. As Colonel Edgerly's name indicates, his father must have been a Democrat and an ardent admirer of Martin Van Buren, who was Vice President of the United States when Colonel Edgerly was born and who, four years later, became President. Colonel Edgerly was a Democrat, too, and was aggressive in the field of politics, as in all else that he undertook. But, fortunately for the Massachusetts Mutual, there were not then enough other Democrats in New Hampshire. In spite of the lively run which Colonel Edgerly made, as the Democratic candidate for the New Hampshire governorship in 1882, he was defeated by 500 votes. What might have been either the end or the prolonged interruption of his insurance career was averted.

In Springfield Colonel Edgerly avoided nomination for public office. This was possibly in part because there were again too few other Democrats, but chiefly because his insurance career opened new vistas of service and of recognized leadership among the insurance men of the country. The growth of the Company during the nine years of his presidency was remarkable. On January 1, 1886, a month before his election, the gross assets of the Company were $8,108,754, the surplus to policyholders was $632,635 and the insurance in force, represented by 15,621 policies, was $37,965,000. At the time of his death in 1895, the gross assets of the Company had increased to $15,653,000, the surplus to policyholders to $1,143,600 and the insurance in force had more than doubled, having increased to $89,878,000. Yet during his term of service the Company did not absorb all of Colonel Edgerly's virile energies. He

70

The Home Office staff in the early nineties.

quickly became a recognized leader in the community. He was a many-sided man who added social grace and marked personal charm to great energy and high ability.

It is clear that the forcefulness which Colonel Edgerly had shown as a young man in winning a place for himself in insurance ranks was too much a part of him not to be in evidence, as the figures have shown, when he became president of the Company. But other forms of expression than those of mere growth are significant both of Colonel Edgerly and of the Company's history. It was a time when, through tontine policies or other doubtful schemes and practices, mere size had become too much the measure of advertised success in certain insurance circles.

71

The energy which Colonel Edgerly had shown in that early episode, in which he secured eight applications between sunset and sunrise in a little New Hampshire town, did not lead him, when he took command of the Massachusetts Mutual, to inaugurate a campaign of uncontrolled expansion. On the contrary, although the business of the Company grew and multiplied while he was at the helm, it was always a growth which was carefully regulated and, from time to time, held rigidly within predetermined limits. Again and again, in the annual statements sent to policyholders and shown to new prospects, Colonel Edgerly emphasized the value of doing business, so far as the Massachusetts Mutual was concerned, at the lowest possible expense ratio. That, to him, was a better test of a life insurance company than mere bigness. He was vigilant as to economy in administration and convinced of the value of that economy as an advertising asset.

Because of the tendencies of those times, which were to have their climax in the Hughes-Armstrong investigation, certain of Colonel Edgerly's annual reports are especially worth quotation. In the Company's 40th annual report, dated January 1892, he declared:

I wish to enter my protest against the pernicious custom on the part of some agents of changing or undertaking to change policies that have been placed in first-class companies to others. It is the new business that costs. When a person has taken a policy in a first-class company, and is approached by the agent of a rival company, with inducements to drop his policy and change to another, that agent is not the friend of the insured. The new business thus gained has necessarily to be paid for twice. I desire to say right here that we do not wish any business placed in our Company, by any of our agents, that has been obtained by causing the policyholder to drop an already existing policy in another company doing a legitimate life insurance business. Under no circumstances will we allow any of our agents

Colonel Martin Van Buren Edgerly, third president, 1886-1895.

to seek that kind of business. At the same time we shall undertake to protect our own business, and to prevent the policies in this Company from being changed to any other. There is business enough for all, and we shall strive to increase ours gradually and on conservative principles, and to add to the Company's strength, year by year; beyond that we have no desire.

Another evil, and a very expensive one, in connection with life insurance, is the practice of hiring agents already under contract with other companies, either by offering inducements or by making them dissatisfied with the company for which they are working. This practice, and that of changing policies from one company to another, as alluded to above, are two evils in the business that can be entirely eliminated if each company will take the matter in hand. We propose to stand by the principles here laid down, and to do our part, at least, toward removing these objectionable features of the business. With these two evils remedied, new business can be written at less cost than it has been, *and the insuring public would get the benefit of the saving.*

The full importance of what Colonel Edgerly had to say about hiring agents away from one company to another can hardly be appreciated without reference to other descriptions of that evil and the proportions it had reached. Burton J. Hendrick in "The Story of Life Insurance" has described the practice, far too prevalent at that time, of offering extravagant inducements, salaries or commissions, to agents who were thought to be capable of adding to the swollen figures of insurance in force. Sooner or later, all such extravagances had to come out of the pocket of the policyholder. That was what Colonel Edgerly was fighting. Against it he was ranging the Massachusetts Mutual and its reputation for careful, economical management.

The panic of 1893 caused Colonel Edgerly to say in the report of January, 1894:

It has been predicted that it would be impossible for a Massachusetts company to pass through such a panic and pay cash surrender values under our law. The condition of our Company at the close

74

of the year is the best answer to that prediction. We have paid out all the money that has been called for in accordance with the law, and yet had cash enough on hand to withstand the double strain that was caused by the depression. The history of the year 1893 demonstrates that no financial institution can be depended on with so much certainty as a well managed life insurance company. No panic more severe in duration and effects will probably ever be witnessed than the one we have just passed through. [If he had been alive forty years later Colonel Edgerly would have admitted that he was a better insurance man than prophet.] It was not in any way local, but extended in all its severity to every portion of the country where the Massachusetts Mutual writes business, and, in truth, far beyond.

Colonel Edgerly's last report of January, 1895, said:

The law of Massachusetts, under which cash values are claimable by policyholders at stated times, has been the subject of criticism by companies of other states. It has been said that its effect would be unfavorable, if not dangerous in times of financial disturbance, on account of the large number of withdrawals which would take place. Our experience during the past two years of financial and business depression seems to have effectually answered such criticism. The surrendered insurance of the Massachusetts Mutual during 1893 was but 3 per cent and during 1894 but 3.4 per cent of the amount of insurance in force. It would be hard to imagine a better test of the law than has been furnished by the experience of the past two years. While the cash value of a policy cannot be legally demanded except on an anniversary of the policy date, this Company has not, except in a few cases when it seemed necessary, enforced this feature of the law, but has accommodated its policyholders who wished to surrender, without regard to the anniversary provision. There can be no doubt of the advantage to the policyholder of the provisions of this law, as they enable him to know at all times the exact amount of cash which can be realized should he wish to retire from the Company, or should his necessities compel such a step on his part. Those who have been able by a surrender of their policies to obtain needed funds have not failed to express their appreciation of the equitable provisions of the statute, and have been the means of extending its popularity.

75

John A. Hall, fourth president, 1895-1908.

With the succession of John A. Hall to the presidency in 1895, on the sudden death of Colonel Edgerly, the tradition of the "career man" at the head of the Massachusetts Mutual became more firmly established. Mr. Hall had begun in the insurance business at an even earlier age than Colonel Edgerly. It absorbed his energies and abilities to such a degree that when he died suddenly on a trip to Europe it was said of him in the *Springfield Republican,* with reference to those who had been presidents of the Massachusetts Mutual up to that time, that Mr. Hall was "the best of them all."

Some measure of Mr. Hall's devotion to his work, the Massachusetts Mutual being literally his passion, may be found in the fact that for twenty years after his election as secretary he took no vacation. Even after his election as president he sought little relief from his burdens. It was the irony of fate that while on a vacation, which was apparently almost forced upon him by the directors, he died suddenly in London, on September 3, 1908. Only a few weeks later, the Company's second Home Office building, erected on the site of the old Foot Block, and to the plans of which he had given infinite pains, was ready for occupation.

Mr. Hall was born December 17, 1840, in Saratoga Springs, N. Y., where he went to school. In 1856, at the age of sixteen, he went to work in the grocery store of his uncle, Ezra Hall. Two years later he went to the Wheeler and Wilson sewing machine factory in Bridgeport, Connecticut, where he remained for two and one half years at a wage of 50 cents a day. At about the time of the outbreak of the Civil War he came to Springfield, joined the force of the United States Armory and remained there for four years, retiring as an assistant inspector. In 1865 he began his insurance career as an agent for a New York life insurance company. In 1872 he

77

Marcus P. Knowlton, Chief Justice of the Massachusetts Supreme Court and a director of the Company, 1900-1918.

78

became the Springfield general agent of the Massachusetts Mutual, his office being in the same old Foot Block where the Company had begun its existence. In 1877 Mr. Hall was made a director of the Company and in 1880 he became superintendent of agencies. The next year he became its secretary, although a minority of the directors favored the continuation in that office of Avery J. Smith. In 1895, on the death of Colonel Edgerly, he was elected president and no thought of the election of anyone else seems to have entered the mind of any director.

In spite of his intense devotion to the Massachusetts Mutual, Mr. Hall was not a man who permitted himself to be narrowed by one interest, absorbing though it was. He had not gone to college, but it was said of him that few businessmen had read more widely in science, history and general literature. Not only was he well informed in many lines, but he was of a responsive nature and, in the best sense, an unusually agreeable talker. The large investment operations of the Company made him well known in financial circles in New York, where he was looked on with appreciative respect. In Springfield he had given the municipality good service in his earlier years and he was regarded, not less so because of his unfailing courtesy, as one of the community's notable assets. His keen sympathy with those under him and his special interest in young men enabled him, with his minute understanding of the insurance business, to command an exceptional degree of loyalty from both the Home Office and the agency force. Something of the quality of his mind is suggested by the fact that he was both a studious and an expert chess player. It was told of him that he was once playing chess at his club when a friend came in who could find no opponent. Mr. Hall suggested that if the friend would set out a board back of him he would play two games at once. This he did and with success, accomplishing one of the familiar exhibition feats of the chess masters.

The Spanish-American War of 1898, which came during Mr. Hall's administration, left little mark in the records of the Massachusetts Mutual. In the Company's forty-seventh annual report of January 1, 1899, President Hall said: "It cannot be definitely stated at this time just how much the war will increase the death payments of the Company, but probably from sixty to seventy-five thousand dollars." Listed among the 480 death claims paid in 1898 for a total of $1,371,330 were eighteen to "Army Men (Officers and Men)" for $64,581.

The war with Spain was short and its proportions were small compared with the Civil War and the two World Wars. At the time, few suspected its historical significance as the starting point from which the progress of the United States as a world power has since been measured. Its direct effect on the Massachusetts Mutual as reported by President Hall was unimportant. Yet the Company, like all our institutions, was inevitably caught in the stream of events which the war with Spain, like an opened sluice gate, set in full current. It paved the way for the spectacular career of Theodore Roosevelt, whose influence on both national affairs and international relations was to be memorable.

In some of the events of the Spanish War the Company had a local interest, even if they figured neither in its records nor its operations. The experience of the Second Massachusetts Regiment of the National Guard, recruited largely in Springfield, bore tragic testimony to inefficiency in military preparations at the same time that it was a monument to the courage of the men in uniform. Because they were

80

Battleship OREGON *in the Straits of Magellan
on her way to the war with Spain.*

equipped only with ammunition using the old-fashioned black powder, the smoke of which marked the American lines too accurately, the men of the Second Massachusetts were ordered to hold their own fire at El Caney while under the fire of the enemy. To that was added, as the further price of inefficiency, an appalling number of deaths from camp diseases.

In one spectacular event of the war with Spain the Company had a neighborly as well as common patriotic interest. This was the famous voyage of seventy-nine days and 14,700 miles of the battleship *Oregon* from Puget Sound around South America to join the American fleet that was waiting in the Caribbean Sea to do battle with the Spanish ships under Admiral Cervera. The commander of the *Oregon* on that voyage was Admiral Charles Edgar Clark who, although

81

born in Vermont and appointed to the naval academy from that state, had close associations, through marriage, with Western Massachusetts. Over in Worcester, meanwhile, they were storing silver and other heirlooms which some of the best families in Boston anxiously felt should not be left to the mercies of hostile cannon if the Spanish fleet suddenly appeared in Boston harbor.

When the one-sided battle was finally fought off Santiago harbor July 3, 1898, the strength of the Spanish ships proved to have been grossly overestimated. Although the *Oregon* was therefore hardly needed for the complete destruction of the Spanish fleet, the significance of her voyage, followed breathlessly by an anxious nation, was obvious. It was one of the chief influences leading to the construction of the Panama Canal, one of the great engineering achievements of our age and a monument to its chief engineer, General Goethals. It is also a great testimonial to advances in public sanitation—without which its construction might have been impossible—directed by General Gorgas. The procedure involved in the acquisition of the Canal Zone was, in some respects, less fortunate and long handicapped our relations with the nations to the south of us.

The Company's second building, to which Mr. Hall gave such care and thought but which he did not live to see it occupy, did not long remain adequate for the growth for which he had laid broader foundations. Within twenty years, a much shorter time than the first building had served, it was outgrown. It was recognized, in spite of some opinion that its height set an undesirable trend in a small city, as representing, in the care, quality and design of its construction, the dignity which the Company had won. It was of eight stories, cost approximately $750,000 and was distinguished both by

*The Rough Riders, led by "Teddy" Roosevelt,
charge the Spaniards.*

its simple stone exterior and its white marble-lined corridors.
Its interior converted to other purposes, and known today as
the "1200 Main Street Building," it is still one of the landmarks of Springfield's business section.

The Company took its character not only from the four
presidents elected during its first half century, but also from
other men of strong personality who filled lesser offices. The
first medical examiner, Dr. Alfred Lambert, who had lent
George W. Rice invaluable support in the founding of the
Company, was a physician of marked ability and distinguished presence who had transferred his practice to Springfield from New York. After serving until 1868 he was
succeeded, until 1880, by Dr. David P. Smith, on whose
death in the latter year, Dr. Lambert resumed the post of
medical examiner for five years more. Dr. Smith, who also

Dr. Alfred Lambert, first medical examiner.

served on the board of directors for nine years, became one of the legendary figures in the history of the Company as well as in that of the surrounding community.

In addition to his private practice and his service to the Massachusetts Mutual, Dr. Smith lectured at the Yale Medical School, where he was regarded with great admiration. He was, in some respects, in advance of the medical science of his time. He had been the chief medical officer of the Army of the Potomac and in later years was described as the best of all the army doctors. He was a man of great kindness. It is also recalled that he stuttered and that, more than occasionally, he swore. In fact, the swearing was an antidote to the stuttering; in his case a "damn" relieved the pent-up words. Up in the hilltop town of Blandford, on the edge of the Berkshires, where Springfield's pure and abundant water is stored in the deep Cobble Mountain reservoir, one of many stories of Dr. Smith is especially treasured.

In days long before the automobile made Blandford easily accessible to members of the Massachusetts Mutual's staff for summer vacations, one of the town worthies, during the harvest season, fell out of an apple tree and dislocated a shoulder. Dr. Smith was summoned and, by horse and buggy, made the slow, steep journey up to Blandford's heights from the Westfield Valley. On his arrival he found the unfortunate farmer seated in the kitchen, a shawl thrown over him, and in something of a stupor, either from pain or the generous alcoholic quota given for its relief. Taking off his coat, Dr. Smith resorted to the usual technique in the effort to restore the shoulder to its proper place and function. But the shoulder was stubborn and nothing happened. Then Dr. Smith went into action. Off went his vest and when he pulled it was with all his force. There was a sudden snap.

85

"T't'there," stuttered Dr. Smith, panting from exertion, "t't'there, d'd'd—n you!" Just as suddenly the farmer came to life while a new pain shot through him. "There, d—n *you!*" he shouted in reply. "That shoulder's been out for years. It's the other one I hurt today." For once the joke was on the medical examiner of the Massachusetts Mutual, although Dr. Smith, among his many attributes, had a reputation as a practical joker himself.

After the interlude of five years through which Dr. Lambert, on the death of Dr. Smith, resumed his service as chief medical examiner of the Massachusetts Mutual, that office was taken over, on Dr. Lambert's death in 1885, by Dr. Frederick W. Chapin. It was again a distinguished succession. Although of markedly different characteristics of manner from Dr. Smith, the position which Dr. Chapin came to occupy, as the outstanding physician in the community, was similar. Strikingly handsome, with his grey hair and closely trimmed beard, he was a figure to remember and his courtesy made the remembrance one to cherish—even, it was said, by those whose applications for life insurance he was forced to reject. He had graduated from the College of Physicians and Surgeons in New York in 1873 and had come to Springfield to practice in 1875. After Dr. Chapin had served for seventeen years as chief medical examiner of the Massachusetts Mutual, giving most conscientious attention to his duties, the office of medical director was created in 1902. Dr. Chapin was made its first occupant, holding it until his sudden death in December 1910. In 1902 he had been made a director of the Company.

It must sometimes have been difficult for Dr. Chapin, as it evidently was for Dr. Lambert and Dr. Smith before him, to combine attendance at directors' meetings with the urgent

Dr. David P. Smith, second medical examiner.

demands of private medical practice. But a gradual shift in the hour of holding meetings of the board served to make attendance somewhat easier for its medical members as well as to reflect the changing customs of the years. In the Company's very early history board meetings were held, generally if not invariably, at what would now seem the awkward hour of 7:30 in the evening. That could not have been too good a time for physicians accustomed to holding evening office hours. Still less was it a favorable time, if one may judge by the record of attendance, for a hard-fighting Civil War editor, like Samuel Bowles of the *Springfield Republican,* who probably was often getting launched on a slashing editorial on his political opponents, due to be printed in tomorrow morning's paper, just when his fellow insurance directors were sitting down to consider new policy forms and to authorize the payment of death claims. But gradually the appointed hours of board meetings receded into daylight. It was a process which reversed the turning of the clock. Evening gave way to late afternoon, late afternoon to earlier afternoon and now, one hundred years after the founding, to forenoon.

One of the factors which accelerated the change of hours seems to have been the desire for the informal discussions across the table which, during the Company's second quarter century, were reflected in President Bond's invitations to the directors to dine with him when their formal deliberations were over. It was set forth in the minutes, in the record of Mr. Bond's hospitality at the old Massasoit House, once nationally famous for its food, that it became desirable to fix an earlier hour for convening the board. The declared purpose was to give the board full time to consider all matters presented to it before it attacked Mr. Bond's various provi-

88

Dr. Frederick W. Chapin, first medical director.

sions for the inner man. Today the process of reversing the clock has gone so far that such informal, but valuable, meetings of the board precede, instead of follow, its formal sessions and are held across the dinner table the night before.

Like the hours of its meetings, the composition of the Massachusetts Mutual's directorate has changed also, but not in the same measure. The original board of directors, like its successors for some years afterward, was composed of Springfield men. That reflected the impulse of the Company's founding. They included lawyers, merchants, manufacturers, bankers and physicians who were among the leaders of the local community. Gradually choices were made from further afield. When, in 1887, the change was made from monthly meetings of the board to quarterly meetings, it became easier to reach out for a portion of the board's membership and to make it more representative of the growing body of those who, as policyholders, were and are the Company's owners. The laws of Massachusetts require that all directors shall be policyholders and that "two thirds of the directors shall always be residents of the Commonwealth." Operating under these requirements, men of proven business experience have been chosen to the board, not only from other parts of Massachusetts, but from outside the state. They have been ready to give the time to come to the board's meetings from Baltimore, Chicago and other comparably distant places, but the core of the directorate has continued to be found in Springfield.

Another striking figure, whose identification with the Massachusetts Mutual began in its second quarter century, was Colonel Henry M. Phillips. Though short of stature he was handsome as men seldom are. With his imperial and flowing mustache he was reminiscent, despite his controlled

90

and restrained manner, of an older day—the day of "Fighting Phil" Kearny, the one-armed *beau sabreur* of the Civil War who rode the charge with his reins in his teeth. Colonel Phillips, too, had served in the cavalry and near the close of the war, although still in his teens, had been brevetted captain for "gallant conduct." His higher military title had come to him through later service on the staff of Governor William B. Washburn of Massachusetts.

Colonel Phillips was as good a Republican as Colonel Edgerly was a Democrat. He went to the Legislature from Springfield, became the city's mayor for three years from 1883 and then its postmaster in 1890. In 1893 he was elected state treasurer and was re-elected in 1894. But in 1895 he resigned that office to become, on the choice of President Hall, secretary of the Massachusetts Mutual. He had already taken a keen and active interest in the Company's affairs for some years as a member of its board. One of the directions in which he especially turned that interest was toward its investments. He went to Kansas and other Western agricultural states to study the Company's farm mortgages. He reported them to be sound and endorsed the investment policy which they represented, provided they continued to be carefully selected. For a number of years the results, little or no interest being in default, amply justified his finding. But, around the turn of the century, when agriculture had fallen on less prosperous times, farm mortgages ceased to invite the placement of the Company's funds.

Colonel Phillips continued, however, to be one of the varying group of officers and directors—including such successful Springfield businessmen as Lyman W. Besse and Andrew B. Wallace—who then made periodic tours of one section or another of the country to inspect the carefully chosen business properties, mortgages on which have long been and continue to be one of the Company's chief forms of investment. The diligence with which business conditions and local developments were studied on these tours is indicated by a report to the directors on October 23, 1912. A committee, consisting of the president and other directors, had visited Oklahoma City, capital of the newly admitted state of Oklahoma. They reported it to be a beautiful city. They added that it was already distinguished by fine improvements. But they cautiously concluded that the time had not quite arrived to make mortgage loans on Oklahoma properties. Today, the Massachusetts Mutual looks back on a long record of satisfactory investments in Oklahoma City mortgages.

When President Hall died in 1908, Colonel Phillips, who had been elected vice president in 1904, declined, on account of failing health, to be considered as Mr. Hall's successor. He declared himself in favor of William W. McClench. Shortly afterward, on January 1, 1909, Colonel Phillips resigned as vice president, but continued as a director until his death March 2, 1911.

*St. Gaudens' statue of Deacon Samuel Chapin,
one of Springfield's early worthies.*

CHAPTER V

A Clean Bill of Health

THE PRESIDENCY of John A. Hall was marked not only by the
Massachusetts Mutual's notable growth and the construction
of its second Home Office building but by a tempest in the
field of insurance. When the tempest was over many sensa-
tional matters had been reported in the press, some great
insurance companies had been beneficially reorganized in
their management, and new laws governing the insurance
business were on the statute books of the state of New York,
where the storm had broken, and on those of most of the
other states of the Union. Thanks largely to Charles Evans
Hughes, who directed the historic investigation in New

93

York which made him a national figure, life insurance was put upon a better and firmer basis.

Years later Mr. Hughes himself gave testimony to the change that had taken place. In the meantime the extraordinary public career, which began with his searching examination of insurance witnesses, had given to his voice the weight of great prestige. He had been governor of New York and he had failed by only the narrowest margin to become President of the United States. He had then become secretary of state and the outstanding cabinet figure in the Harding administration. Later, in 1930, on appointment by President Hoover, he was to become chief justice of the United States Supreme Court. The insurance business could have asked for no higher endorsement than that which it received when Mr. Hughes declared on December 9, 1926, at the twentieth anniversary convention of the Association of Life Insurance Presidents:

> I am not here to review the past save as I am permitted to congratulate you upon the unparalleled growth and soundness of the life insurance enterprise. During the last twenty years the amount of insurance in force and the invested funds of your companies have vastly grown. This expansion, it is most gratifying to observe, has been achieved with wise conservatism in management, without undue expenditures in obtaining business, and with the returns to policyholders that are consistent with safety. I believe there is no safer or better-managed business in our country than yours.

In the proceedings of the Armstrong-Hughes investigation the Massachusetts Mutual was in no way a direct party. Yet, by contrast, it was a beneficiary. For, except in a few minor details and technicalities, its organization and its practices proved to be in strict conformity with the legislation affecting life insurance which grew out of the investigation. There was no need for it to amend or abandon such unfortunate practices as those which the investigation revealed. Such practices had never been permitted to creep into its operation. The ideals of the founders and their successors, reinforced by what Elizur Wright succeeded in having written into the laws of Massachusetts, gave the Massachusetts Mutual the benefit of a clean bill of health.

It is worth while to describe something of the contrast by which, as a result of the Armstrong-Hughes investigation, the Massachusetts Mutual then benefited. President Edgerly, in his forceful reports, from which quotations have previously been made, had strongly expressed himself on some of the extravagant practices which, after his death, were to lead to the investigation. Among its causes were the various adaptations of the once famous tontine or deferred-dividend policies which the New York laws of 1906 forbade and which the Massachusetts Mutual had never issued.

As originally devised by Lorenzo Tonti, from whom such policies got their name, the tontine was a scheme for raising money for the government of Louis XIV of France in the 17th century. Under this scheme subscription lists were opened to French citizens. Each person who subscribed a specified sum was placed in a class depending on his age. The interest on the aggregate sum subscribed by the members of any class was divided each year among the survivors. As the number of survivors was diminished by death their proportionate share of the annual interest steadily increased. When an individual became the sole survivor of his class, the income paid to him each year represented the interest on all the original subscriptions and was many times his own contribution. The last beneficiary of the first tontine which the French government

95

*In 1908 the Company's second Home Office building
tops Springfield's sky line.*

set up in 1669 did not die until 1726. In that year she received the equivalent of $15,000 against the $60 which she had originally put in. But, from the standpoint of the government, the scheme had the advantage that, when the last survivor died, there was then no further obligation. The subscription had, in effect, been paid off.

During the 17th and 18th centuries, following the successful introduction of Tonti's scheme, Europe witnessed a tontine craze almost as extensive as the stock jobbing schemes which culminated in the bursting of the South Sea Bubble in 1720. Unlike the first tontine of Louis XIV, many of these later tontines were not honestly conducted and the popularity of the scheme waned. It had a new lease of life in the United States when in a new form it was revived in the tontine insurance policy in 1868.

Like other insurance policies, a tontine policy required the payment of an annual premium and promised the payment of the amount insured on the death of the policyholder. But it had two special features. If the policyholder failed to pay any premium on its due date, he forfeited all right to the policy's value. Second, no dividends were payable until the end of a period of years, the so-called "tontine period"—usually twenty years, sometimes ten or fifteen years. These two features were responsible for the piling up of large funds in the treasury of the insurance company. The postponement of dividends and the imposition of total forfeiture on lapsed policies meant that the amounts which would otherwise have been distributed to policyholders as dividends, or paid out in the form of cash values, accumulated in the hands of the company throughout the tontine period. Purchasers of these policies were promised that these accumulations would be distributed at the end of

97

the tontine period to those who survived and maintained their policies in force. Obviously, as long as the plan was operated under these conditions it was advantageous to those who maintained their policies and lived to the end of the tontine period, and disadvantageous to those who died or lapsed their policies before the completion of that period.

Since the tontine policy was a contract of life insurance, it was basically an instrument for the protection of the breadwinner. However, its character in this respect was materially compromised by the marked gambling features it incorporated. A man's family was protected in the event of his death and he himself would reap a large reward *if* he were among the fortunate few who were able to run the gauntlet of hard times, carelessness and misfortune. But there was a very strong probability that he himself might be among the unlucky ones who lost everything, since at the outset no individual could be sure that he would be among the winners. That was the gamble. It is not to be wondered at that the tontine policy had a tremendous appeal at a time when the speculative instincts of a youthful Nation, encouraged by all the temptations of almost untapped natural resources, were under probably less restraint than ever before or since.

In practice, the exaction of total forfeiture on any default in premium payments came to be a handicap in persuading prospects to take out such policies. In consequence the forfeiture provision was modified so that dividends only were forfeited in the event of death or lapse. So modified, the tontine policy became known as the "semi-tontine," or by the more popular designation, the "deferred-dividend" policy. In the 80's the volume of insurance terminating by surrender or lapse was about one-half the amount of new business being written. Glittering inducements were offered in soliciting for deferred-dividend policies. The estimates of dividends to be distributed, at the end of the ten, fifteen or twenty-year periods, were exceedingly high.

With the aid of intensely vigorous promotion, some of it of the kind that President Edgerly protested against, the sale of deferred-dividend policies grew to enormous proportions and advanced the companies which offered them to the positions of leadership in the insurance field. But in the 90's some chickens came home to roost. The estimates of dividends to be distributed were not pledges fixed by contract and the policyholders who expected them, but failed to receive them, were disappointed. The reasons for this poor showing were chiefly two. One was extravagance [again one of President Edgerly's targets] in the race for new business. The other was the careless, not to say reckless, handling in some instances of these funds.

Such practices, including the use, in some cases, of what were popularly known as "slush funds" employed to influence legislation, came in for severe scrutiny during the Armstrong-Hughes investigation. The new laws which were enacted in consequence of the investigation prohibited the issuance of these semi-tontine, deferred-dividend policies, and imposed limits on expenses incurred for new business as well as on the amount of new business to be issued in a calendar year.

The Massachusetts Mutual, if one may judge from the annual reports of President Edgerly and President Hall, was never tempted to enter the field of deferred-dividend policies. If it had been tempted it would still have been prevented by the Massachusetts laws which Elizur Wright had had a hand in getting passed. In the year of the Armstrong-Hughes investigation, the *Chicago Tribune* editorially declared: "Even if federal supervision of life insurance companies is constitutional, about which there is great doubt, it cannot be made any more vigilant or effective than the control now exercised by the insurance department of the state of Massachusetts, which is admitted to be the model for all the world." So the Massachusetts Mutual, like other companies chartered in Massachusetts, profited by comparisons which were drawn by magazine and newspaper writers. At one time it seems to have been expected that a representative of the Massachusetts Mutual would be called on to testify in the Armstrong-Hughes investigation. That this was not done seems to have been due to a realization that it would result in no disclosures such as those which made the investigation a continuing sensation.

Although the tontine insurance scheme was unfortunate in various ways it had its comic side. With the aid of such spelling as Artemus Ward made fashionable in an earlier time, "Samuel Sharkey" held the tontine scheme up to biting ridicule in a series of burlesque letters to the *Springfield Republican*. As previously suggested "Samuel Sharkey" may have been Oscar B. Ireland, the Massachusetts Mutual's actuary through many years. These were letters written from a mythical place in Illinois called "Bourbonville." They portrayed "the Rise, Progress and Fall of the celebrated Canteen Assurance Society."

In these letters it was pitiably set forth by "Samuel Sharkey" how he had finally been refused more credit for more whiskey at the local emporium. The inspiration then came to him to start the "Canteen Association," the name

100

being an obvious play upon "tontine." To those invited to join the association and contribute to its support:

> We stated that a canteen grosery was a purely benevolent project to give to its members an opportunity to provide in their youth for a sure supply of likker in their old age. Members were required to contribute twenty-five cents a week, which would be expended joodishously, but firmly, in a new corn-whisky, at the lowest cash price. This whisky should be put into the canteen barrel, and there stay for a month. At the expiration of a month, the likker is divided among the survivin members.
>
> The ignorant populis had some trouble to understand how they wos to be benefited by this process, and I made it clear to them. In the first place, half of our original members will either die or get tired and resign before the month is up, and the shares of sich become the property of them who stick. In other life insurances the death of a member is agin the company; in the canteen company its in the company's favor.

The sad story of the "Canteen Association" at "Bourbonville" was continued until, the month having expired, the contributing members appeared at a formal meeting and demanded their rights and their "likker." When it developed that the "likker" had all been consumed by the officers, the members made it clear, with some physical emphasis, that they were less than satisfied. After having reflected upon the rude treatment he had received as president and chief consumer, Mr. "Sharkey" philosophically observed in conclusion:

> I have still faith in the Canteen idea, and shel try it agin somewhere else. The trouble with us this time, wos in making the Canteen period too short. We should hev made it a year at least, so that no enquiry cood hev been made until we wos prepared to hev enquiries made. The tontines (from whom I got my noshen), put off their period ten years, which is sensible and a safe time. Then I shel mix it some other way with some other system, so that in times uv difficulty one kin play into the other's hands.

101

William W. McClench, fifth president, 1908-1928.

One very positive advantage, aside from the reforms it necessitated and the advertisement of better-managed companies to which it contributed, came from the Armstrong-Hughes investigation. It produced in the public mind a clearer understanding of the few and very simple fundamental principles on which life insurance is based. President Hall in his annual report of December 31, 1907, undoubtedly referring to the Armstrong-Hughes investigation, stated:

The public knows more about life insurance than formerly. The discussion of the subject by legislative committees, insurance departments, and the press, has thrown much light upon the business, and while weak spots have been exposed, the ever-extending service rendered by sound life insurance institutions has been made equally prominent. The day of the speculative deferred-dividend policy has gone by . . . life insurance never deserved better of the public than now, and it is not rash to predict that, under the new order of things brought about by a campaign of reformation and information, it will enjoy in the future a greater popularity than ever.

The presidency of William W. McClench, who followed Mr. Hall, was distinguished by four outstanding developments. The first was the continued growth of the Company. The second was the occupation of a new Home Office building. The third was World War I. The fourth was the construction and occupation of still another Home Office building, which the Company occupies today. The figures at the beginning and end of Mr. McClench's service as president owe something of their impressiveness to the fact that, except for Caleb Rice, his service as president was longer than that of any other president the Massachusetts Mutual has yet had. The Company's assets on December 31, 1908, shortly after he took office in 1908, were $51,121,000 and its insurance in force $227,506,000. When he retired as

103

president in January 1928, becoming chairman of the board, less than ten months before his death, the assets were $289,729,000 and the insurance in force was $1,609,837,000.

Mr. McClench, who came to the Massachusetts Mutual by way of the law, rather than through the ranks of its trained insurance workers, was a man of forceful bearing, vigorous and dignified speech. He would undoubtedly have had a notable career at the bar or on the bench if the insurance business had not drafted him. Born in Chicopee, Massachusetts, on April 6, 1854, Mr. McClench attended the public schools of that city and in 1875 graduated from Tufts College. For two years after graduation he was engaged in teaching school but had already begun to study law. In 1877 he entered the law office of Stearns, Knowlton & Long in Springfield, being admitted to the Hampden County bar in 1878. That law office was one of the most famous in the history of Western Massachusetts. George M. Stearns is remembered as a wit as well as a brilliant lawyer. Marcus P. Knowlton became a distinguished chief justice of the Massachusetts Supreme Court as well as a director of the Massachusetts Mutual. Charles L. Long was noted for many years as an outstanding judge of probate.

In 1893 Mr. McClench formed a partnership with Frederick H. Gillett, who went to Congress as a representative, became speaker and later United States senator. This partnership continued until 1898, when Mr. McClench retired from private practice. In 1894 he had made his first connection with the Massachusetts Mutual as assistant to Judge Gideon Wells, who was at that time the Company's counsel. On the death of Judge Wells in 1898, Mr. McClench succeeded him as counsel, was elected a director in 1899 and six years later was made second vice president.

104

When John A. Hall died in 1908 Mr. McClench was elected to succeed him.

Mr. McClench's legal ability and impressive manner when speaking from any platform were not unaccompanied by a sense of humor. He would have been the first to admit, although also with just indignation, that, as counsel for the Company, he had once been bested in the courtroom by a famous figure. She was Hetty Green, the celebrated miser whose peculiar methods of protecting and adding to her great wealth both amused and shocked the Nation over a long period.

Eight years before Mr. McClench's election as president, the Massachusetts Mutual had received a tax bill of $1,105 for real estate in Chicago. What followed was at least valuable as a warning. The bill was paid without certifying the property. Later the Company received a second bill. A protest was at once made that the Company had both the receipted bill and its cancelled check to prove that payment had been made in full. Then the facts came out. The Chicago tax collector advised the Company that, through the error of a clerk, it had been sent a bill for taxes that were due on property which belonged to Hetty Green.

Efforts to recover the amount paid were made through friendly negotiations. Mr. McClench and another official of the Company called on Mrs. Green at her New York bank. They explained what had happened through the error of the Chicago clerk. The atmosphere of the interview seemed to be agreeable. Mr. McClench and his companion left with what they thought was a verbal acknowledgment of the debt, to be followed by Mrs. Green's check. But no check came, in spite of endless correspondence.

Finally, the Company brought suit against Hetty Green.

105

The presentation of the case took several days. In the end, the judge ruled "that Mrs. Hetty Green was under no legal obligation to refund the tax money to the Insurance Company." The judge added, however, that whatever obligation existed was moral. "That," exclaimed Hetty Green triumphantly to her lawyer, "is sound law. I'll take the moral responsibility of not paying."

In 1912, while Mr. McClench was president, one of the striking events in American political history took place within a stone's throw of the Company's Home Office. From time to time, in campaign years and in between, our Presidents had stopped briefly in Springfield. In June, 1899, President McKinley had made a New England tour. He had come down the Connecticut River from Holyoke in the little excursion steamer "Mascot" and from her deck had greeted the crowd which assembled on the river's banks to see him land. That had been followed by a more formal welcome and short presidential speech from a reviewing stand in front of the city hall.

The visit of President Taft in 1912 was very different from that of President McKinley. It marked the bursting into full and violent flame of the feud which had been smouldering for more than two years between him and his predecessor in the White House, Theodore Roosevelt. It was at Springfield, from a temporary stand erected on Court Square back of the old First Church, that Taft chose to make his first speech openly replying to the man who, four years before, had been the chief instrument of his election. Later that same day Taft spoke at Worcester and, in the evening, before a mass meeting in Boston. But it was at Springfield that he angrily broke the silence which for many months he had painfully maintained under

President William McKinley visits Springfield by water.
He stands at the extreme right on the upper deck.

mounting attack. The clerks of the Massachusetts Mutual might almost have heard him from the windows of the Home Office building, not far from the speaker's stand.

President McKinley's visit to Springfield in an off-election year had been relatively non-political, while President Taft's was the opening gun in one of the bitterest battles in all our political history. But there was another difference. When McKinley came it was still the age of the horse. When Taft came thirteen years later, the transition to the automobile era—in which Springfield had had a special part through original invention and early manufacture—was in full swing. Taft alighted from his special railroad car in the yards only a short distance from his speaking stand.

But he was transported even that short distance by automobile. The omnipresent secret service guards, who both precede and follow every President, stood on the running boards. From that and other cars they scanned the crowd, in which fellow members of their force were mingling, for dangerous cranks. Fortunately for Taft and for Springfield's reputation they found none.

On April 1, 1913, a year after President Taft's fighting speech in Springfield, appeared the first issue of *The Radiator*, the Company's monthly magazine. Since then it has served increasingly as a medium for news concerning the personnel of the Home Office and of the agencies throughout the country, but especially for the discussion of a wide range of insurance problems. As part of that discussion, the Company's successive presidents, beginning with Mr. McClench, who was in office when *The Radiator* was founded, have employed it for messages of many sorts. Other important members of the great co-operative group, representing both the Home Office and the field force, have also contributed to its pages.

The first issue of *The Radiator* was a modest publication of eight pages. Some magazines have radically changed their format in the hope of making a greater popular appeal. It is notable that no such experiments have been made with *The Radiator*. But while its pages remain of the same size, their number has multiplied and their typography has been attractively varied. More especially, they have reflected, with the aid of many illustrations, the personal relations on which the service of life insurance so peculiarly depends.

The Radiator has reported not only the personal and recreational side of agents' conventions and regional meetings, but especially the speeches and reports on subjects of vital common interest which have made those conventions and meetings of permanent value. The high standard which this magazine maintains is indicated by the fact that it has received nine awards of excellence at the annual meetings and exhibits of the Life Insurance Advertisers Association, since it was first entered in these competitions in 1932.

The impact of World War I on life insurance as an institution was very different from that of the war with Spain. The difference was chiefly that of size. Wars had grown, but so had life insurance. Life insurance had come to play a far larger part in the national economy when, in 1917, the United States entered World War I than it had in 1898 when the war with Spain began and was quickly over. But, unfortunately, the scale of modern warfare had grown even faster. The phrase "total war," now so familiar, had not gained currency in 1917. Yet the forces which have since made it the great problem of the survival of modern civilization were already making it a fact.

This situation, as it affected life insurance, was made more and more apparent between August, 1914, when World War I began and April, 1917, when Woodrow Wilson called on America to bear arms because "God helping her, she can do no other." It was a situation which Alexander T. Maclean, then the new assistant actuary of the Massachusetts Mutual and later its eighth president, analyzed in the April, 1917, issue of *The Radiator*. Mr. Maclean, who had his early life insurance experience in Scotland before coming to this country, described with care and precision the experience of the British companies up to that period of World War I. He defined with clarity the problem before them, or before the British government, at the time when, with the British advance on the Somme, the fighting entered its more sanguinary phases and the losses multiplied.

One of the most interesting phases of Mr. Maclean's discussion of the inter-relation between life insurance and the risks of war service emphasized the falling rate of death from disease as reflected in the statistics of the wars of the nineteenth century. He recalled that in the Mexican War of 1846 the combined death rate from wounds and disease for the duration of the war, a period of seventeen months, had been 118 per thousand but that the death rate from disease alone had been 104 per thousand. In the Civil War the average annual death rate was approximately 110 per thousand but deaths from disease, although still high, had fallen to sixty-nine per thousand. In this connection he also emphasized that "not all of the effects of war are felt during the actual war period." It was, he declared, with the physical condition of the population that a life insurance company was most concerned. Therefore, the fact must be faced that for many years after a war has ended "there is bound to be a lessened vitality in the Nation due to the very great many citizens who have done actual war service and who, although coming out of the war without serious damage, have nonetheless suffered a decrease in constitutional force."

Mr. Maclean pointed out that prior to 1914 conditions in this country and Great Britain had been very much the same. About twenty-five years earlier "all policies issued in this country contained limitations as to military and naval service and, even in the most liberal policy, the sum insured was not paid in full should death be the result of such service." These restrictions and limitations were gradually

110

*Trench warfare in World War I. Allied with the Germans
were the cooties, rats and mud.*

eliminated and "most of the policies issued for some years
prior to the present war [World War I] were absolutely
unrestricted." In Great Britain, prior to 1914, "the majority
of recently issued policies were without any limitations as
to military or naval service unless the insured was already
a member of the regular army or navy." On the outbreak
of the war most of the British companies waived "all rights
to collect extra premiums from existing policyholders."
While this action occasioned some criticism, Mr. Maclean
pointed out that "the average age of the policyholders
in any company, which had been in existence for any
length of time, would be such that the majority of the
members would not be available for war service."

But, Mr. Maclean emphasized, "When we come to new
entrants, the case is entirely different. At the inception of

111

a war there will always be a rush of applicants for insurance and these will come in many cases from men who have every intention of volunteering for service. It is not to be expected that any company should accept this almost certain material extra risk without proper consideration, and the experience of the war has shown how inadequate were the first estimates of the proper extra premiums to be charged." Summing up the great service of the British insurance companies up to that time, Mr. Maclean prophetically concluded: "It may perhaps seem that these conditions are not likely to be reproduced in this country, but to the average citizen in Great Britain, war seemed much more remote in the spring of 1914 than it does to us today."

From January to August, 1917, as the war clouds darkened and the storm broke, new policies issued by the Massachusetts Mutual contained war clauses providing protective features for the Company. In August, 1917, a "five-year clause," standard with most companies, was adopted for use with newly issued policies. This clause provided for the payment of such extra premium as the Company might require if the insured entered military or naval service within five years from the policy's date of issue. This extra premium was payable during the continuance of such military service, and if not paid the Company would be liable for only the reserve value of the policy in event the insured died as a result of military service.

Following the armistice in November, 1918, restrictions on military and naval service were made inoperative as to all policies in force and were omitted from all policies being currently issued, except with regard to total and permanent disability coverage.

World War I did not directly affect either the Massachusetts Mutual or other American insurance companies as much as our more recent experience in World War II might lead one to expect. The number of employees who joined the armed forces in the first World War was far exceeded by similar enlistments in the second. The directors, moved no doubt by rumors of sabotage, took out explosion insurance of $400,000 on the Company's building. The Black Tom explosion later gave proof that such apprehensions were not entirely groundless even though an insurance company, located in an interior city, seems in retrospect to have been remote from danger. The Company's war losses up to December 31, 1918, under 315 policies, amounted to $525,746. These included the death claims not only of those in the armed services but also of members of the Red Cross, Y. M. C. A. and other kindred war work organizations.

More serious than World War I in its effect on the life insurance companies, from the standpoint of death losses, was "the severe and widespread epidemic of influenza," as President McClench described it in the Company's annual report of December 31, 1918. "Owing in large part to this cause," he said, "rather than to the war, our mortality experience for the year was less favorable than for many years. But this experience was undoubtedly common to all the life insurance companies of the country." The Company's payments for death losses during 1918, in fact, jumped about 50 per cent. The epidemic took over 400,000 lives in the country as a whole. At its height many who had never seen either an army camp or a field hospital saw the establishment in Springfield of a tented camp for the care of influenza victims.

113

*The graceful campanile dominates Springfield's
municipal group.*

114

On December 31, 1918, out of total assets of $112,662,-000, the Company had $8,112,900 invested in Liberty Loan bonds. This was a great increase over the few thousands the Company had been able similarly to invest in government bonds during the Civil War. But it was to pale almost to insignificance when compared with the huge sums which the Company was to invest in War and Victory bonds in World War II.

World War I also saw the assumption by the government of life insurance for men in the armed forces. This marked a recognition that the problem with all its hazards was beyond the scope of private companies. The attitude of the Massachusetts Mutual as to this action by the government left no room for doubt. It emphasized the fact that the insurance was offered by the government at a low rate and urged all in uniform to take advantage of it. Later, when an overwhelmingly large proportion of the ex-service men allowed their government insurance to lapse, the Company took a strong stand. It urged the ex-service men to reinstate their policies whenever possible. Its representatives were instructed to assist in these reinstatements and to encourage the veterans to keep their government insurance in force. But although so many of the ex-service men did unwisely let their government insurance lapse, it was apparent, from the largely increased business done by the Massachusetts Mutual and other private companies in the years which came immediately after World War I, that experience had served to make the American public alive to the protection and benefits of life insurance as never before.

The present Home Office building of the Massachusetts Mutual is one of Springfield's two outstanding architectural landmarks. The other is the famous municipal group, a unique and successful combination of two Greek temples, one housing the municipal offices and one the municipal auditorium, with an Italian clock tower or campanile rising between them. In contrast to that gifted adaptation of classic design, the Massachusetts Mutual building presents, on the outskirts of the city, a striking example of Georgian architecture of brick and limestone, four stories high and with a frontage of approximately 400 feet. The street frontage of the Company's land is 1,480 feet and its average depth 880 feet. This area of about thirty acres provides a setting of wide, green lawns and massed shrubs such as the building's architectural beauty deserves.

President McClench, in making the first announcement of the plans for the new building in July, 1924, observed: "When we moved into the present eight-story building in 1908, we thought the Home Office would remain there for the next thousand years. We had no conception then of the wonderful growth which the Company was destined to experience. In that year we had about $300,000,000 [his memory somewhat exaggerated the actual figure] in outstanding insurance; today, sixteen years after, the insurance carried by the Company aggregates more than $1,000,000,000. In 1908, the Company wrote $25,000,000 insurance, while last year it wrote $160,000,000. The office force in 1908 numbered 100; now it exceeds 400."

The decision to erect a new type of building on the outskirts of Springfield, where it would have ample space around it for future growth and for the parking of employees' cars, has been amply justified. There are obvious advantages in such a semi-suburban site as compared with the many-storied skyscrapers which, in larger cities, it has

116

been felt necessary to build for insurance uses on more highly taxed land. Some months before the Company's centennial anniversary, it completed a large, harmoniously designed addition to its Home Office building. This addition will provide the space which the Company imperatively needs, with once more a margin for further growth.

The Home Office building represents the best Georgian tradition as transplanted to New England where, in colonial days, that tradition was given such a fortunate expression as to become a definite and important part of the New England scene. The most striking exterior feature is the main entrance with its broad steps and portico of six Ionic columns and classic pediment. Just inside is the impressive yet not exaggerated rotunda which, as the central and pivotal point, shows a richer treatment in both material and design than any other part of the building. The use of marble is here carried further in the floor, columns, and supports of the encircling gallery than elsewhere, while the grilles, gallery railing and clock are of bronze. Corridors are floored with Travertine and asphalt tile and wainscotted with Tennessee marble, which is the marble of the rotunda floor. The general plan of the building is that of a hollow square divided by a central wing, thus forming two interior courts, laid out with evergreens and flowering shrubs, fountains and green and purple flagging. The addition extends what are in effect the two side wings.

The careful planning by Bertrand J. Perry and other officers, before ground was broken for the Massachusetts Mutual building, bears fruit today in the efficiency with which one operation succeeds another in the Company's many and varied departmental activities. These include the issuance of policies, the granting of policy loans, the settlement of death claims, the preparation and mailing of thousands of monthly income checks to policyholders and beneficiaries, and all other types of policyholder service which make up the daily round of Home Office activity.

Massachusetts Mutual policyholders make use, in the depression, of the loan values of their policies.

CHAPTER VI

Through the Depression and War

IT FELL to William H. Sargeant, sixth president of the Massachusetts Mutual, to guide it through the worst years of the great depression. From Mr. Sargeant's election as president on January 25, 1928, Mr. McClench had served as chairman of the board of directors until his death on November 16, 1928. Thus Mr. Sargeant had been less than a year in full command when, in the fall of 1929, the collapse of inflated values on the stock market began the first chapter of what was to become a vast national disaster. Mr. Sargeant was peculiarly fitted, both by character and by experience, to hold his post on the bridge and guide his ship through the storm. It was an ordeal for him, as it was

119

also an opportunity for the Massachusetts Mutual to prove, under extraordinary stress, the value of life insurance as an institution.

It could be said of Mr. Sargeant, with greater truth than of either Colonel Edgerly or Mr. Hall, that he had grown up in the insurance business. One began at twenty-six, the other at twenty-five. Mr. Sargeant began when he was not yet sixteen. Born in Springfield October 5, 1868, he went through the lower public schools, attended high school for only a few months and made a brief trial of a local business school. He then began his long insurance career when he reported for work at the Home Office of the Massachusetts Mutual on June 23, 1884. Insurance was not only his life-work for fifty-one years but, to a large degree, his education.

Shortly after Mr. Sargeant joined the Company he contributed the following to *The Massachusetts Mutual,* then the Company's house organ:

From Our Youngest Contributor

Life insurance is one of the best investments a man can make, especially if he is a married man. When a man has obtained insurance in a reliable life insurance company (the Massachusetts Mutual Life Insurance Company, for instance), he is assured that his family will not want when he is dead. There are plenty of men who when living could not be persuaded to take out any kind of a policy, but if living today could tell you how much they suffered on their death beds thinking of the future of their families when, if they had insured as their friends advised them to do, they could have died without a regret, having done all they could for their wives and children.

A minister once said to a friend when asked what he thought about giving flowers to be placed on a dead friend's coffin, if you have any flowers to give me, give them to me when I am alive and can appreciate them.

120

So it is in mutual life insurance (where the policyholders are the only stockholders) you partake of the buds of the flowers in the way of dividends which are paid every year.

Now, my friend, which are you going to do? Die and leave your family for your friends to support, or are you going to plant your flowers immediately and partake of the fragrance of the buds when you are alive, and when you die you know that the buds will be turned into handsome flowers by your family receiving the face of your policy?

W. H. SARGEANT *(Aged 16)*.

Thirteen clerks and three active officers comprised the whole Home Office staff of the Massachusetts Mutual on the day Mr. Sargeant joined it. The officers were President Bond, John A. Hall, secretary, and Oscar B. Ireland, actuary. Step by step, in Horatio Alger style, the new office boy worked his way up as he familiarized himself with every possible detail of the work. His first notable promotion came in 1900 when he was appointed inspector of agencies and risks. In that capacity he did much traveling to the offices of general agents. When he finally reached the top of the ladder, no president before him had had quite so intimate a knowledge of the field force.

Not only did Mr. Sargeant grow up with the Massachusetts Mutual, but he saw the Massachusetts Mutual grow up with him. For he entered its ranks just before the era of its more rapid and aggressive growth, which began under Colonel Edgerly and was continued under Mr. Hall and succeeding presidents. The Company's statement at the close of 1884, as Mr. Sargeant was mastering his first job, showed assets of $7,553,000, and insurance in force of $34,665,000. The statement at the end of 1935, which almost exactly coincided with his death on December 28 of that year, showed assets of $533,225,000 and insurance in force of $1,851,447,000.

121

William H. Sargeant, sixth president, 1928-1936.

The story of the depression as it affected life insurance, and how the Massachusetts Mutual met the emergency, lacks the sudden and dramatic impact of the Chicago fire of 1871 and the San Francisco earthquake and fire of 1906 on the fire insurance companies. The depression was a disaster whose dimensions grew and grew over a period of many months; it was unlike the flames which swiftly swept block after block and then died down, largely for lack of more buildings to devour. Yet the values which were swept away in the depression, and the shrinking of private property and corporate assets which resulted from it, culminated in aggregate national losses so staggering as to make those of the Chicago and San Francisco fires seem almost trifling in comparison. How greatly our tottering national economy was buttressed and steadied by the life insurance companies has, perhaps, never been adequately told.

In the case of the Massachusetts Mutual the onset and sinister progress of the depression were registered in President Sargeant's reports to the directors. Claims based on death through suicide, like applications for loans based on policies, soon began to increase along with lapses due to inability to meet premiums. Terminations grew so that finally, the writing of new business for a six-month period, as reported by Mr. Sargeant to the directors, was actually less than the insurance which had been terminated by death and otherwise, making the insurance in force on July 1, 1932, less than that in force on January 1, 1932. Then came the swelling stream of defaults on mortgages, and to a lesser degree on bonds, which had been scrutinized with infinite care when originally chosen as proper investments for the Company's funds. The situation called for a cool head and a steady hand.

In November, 1929, following the break in the stock market in October, the Massachusetts Mutual made an average of 222 policy loans (cash loans) per day to its policyholders. The average daily total was $155,000 and the total for the month $3,712,000. This is the largest amount of loans to policyholders the Company has ever made in a single month. In the depth of the depression in 1932 such loans to policyholders reached their maximum for a single year. The number of new loans made in that year rose to 60,117 and their total amount to $26,000,000. From that peak the demand gradually declined, until in 1942, the policy loans made were less than $5,000,000, which could be regarded as normal.

These loans, large though they came to be, were only one item in the service rendered by the Massachusetts Mutual to its policyholders during the period of most acute public need in the Company's first hundred years. Because the need was so great and the crisis, for many persons and families, so desperate, special importance is attached to other figures in the Company's record in the years from 1929 to 1937. Not only did cash loans on policies, to serve such needs as will presently be recalled, reach unprecedented heights, but so also did premium loans made to enable policyholders to keep their policies in force.

In 1929, before the full force of the depression was felt, policy loans, made during the year, rose to $15,500,000 and premium loans to $4,160,000. As already noted, new policy loans reached their peak in 1932 with a total of $26,000,000, but it was not until 1933, when new policy loans had begun to fall off sharply, that new premium loans reached their peak with a total of $11,200,000 and then began a steady, but not sharp, decline. During the nine years from 1929 to

1937 inclusive, total policy loans were $129,230,000 and total premium loans $63,190,000, making the combined total of both forms of loans made by the Company to its policyholders during these years, $192,420,000. For that same period, the primary and much greater service by the Company toward meeting even more vital needs of its policyholders and beneficiaries was represented by payments to them aggregating $448,500,000. This sum was in addition to the loans previously mentioned and represented death benefits, matured endowments, annuity and disability payments, accidental death benefits, cash surrender values, and dividends.

In the case of the Massachusetts Mutual, the service of life insurance had one episode hardly less dramatic than the formal pledges of the sounder fire insurance companies that the Chicago and San Francisco losses would be paid in full. No city was hit harder than Detroit. The closing of the Michigan banks before Washington ordered the general suspension of bank operations throughout the country in March, 1933, was one of the grave developments which finally forced that step at the Capital. In the Detroit area the Massachusetts Mutual had written much insurance and its energetic agency in that city was eager to do all that it could to assist needy policyholders to secure loans on their Massachusetts Mutual policies.

In February, 1933, the governor of Michigan declared a legal holiday for all the banks in the state. His action was approved by the state Legislature as well as by the federal and state banking authorities. Practically all banks in the state closed. This bank holiday was supposed to extend from February 14 to February 21. But many Michigan banks remained closed after the latter date and did not

125

reopen until the national bank holiday, which began on March 4, was declared at an end.

During the Michigan bank holiday the Massachusetts Mutual's Michigan policyholders could not cash its checks. The Company, therefore, sent currency to its agencies in Michigan to take care of applications for policy loans. The total amount sent was over $300,000. In addition, over $100,000 in currency was sent by registered mail, insured, to agencies in other states where banks were closed or on a restricted basis.

Such was the record from the Company's end. What its aid meant to those who needed it most is told in a letter from the Company's agency at Detroit:

Policyholders of the Massachusetts Mutual on the books of the Detroit Agency, some 15,000 in number, remembered that we had told them how our policies would furnish cash to meet emergencies. So they came to us in such streams that it was necessary to have four of our agents appointed deputy sheriffs and carry revolvers, lest there be disorder. When our cash on hand got low, due to disbursements for loans on policies and the withdrawal of dividend accumulations, means had to be devised for increasing our money supply.

A long-distance telephone call to the Home Office revealed our predicament and state of emergency. As requests for loans or dividend withdrawals were made, shipments of cash were forwarded to us by the Company by registered mail, American Express and airplane. We never had one of these requests for money which was intended to buy food, pay hospital bills, meet payrolls, keep children in school, meet mortgage payments on homes, give people transportation money for emergency travel or any other purpose for which cash was needed, which we were unable to fill.

One morning, a coal dealer, with eighteen yards in various sections of the city, telephoned and said the coal supply of many customers had been exhausted while others would soon be in the same dire strait. This included homes, schools, hospitals, factories, and various institutions. Prompt aid was needed to prevent disaster.

126

This policyholder wanted to know if he could get some money in order to have the railroads release many carloads of coal to him which he could not get released on checks, notwithstanding the fact that he had over $200,000 of working capital in the Guardian and First National Banks. We asked if he could get along with $25,000 to $50,000, and he stated that $100,000 would only represent about a ten days' supply, and that he was desperate with telephones ringing in every coal yard office, where people were insisting upon delivery of coal, especially in schools, hospitals, orphanages, and homes where there was illness. It was cold in Detroit.

We told him we would see what we could do to help and telephone him back. Within six hours, we telephoned suggesting that he come down to get his money. We had telephoned the Home Office in Springfield. They, in turn, telephoned the Third National Bank and Trust Company of Springfield; they telephoned the Federal Reserve Bank of Boston; the Federal Reserve Bank of Boston telephoned the Federal Reserve Bank of Chicago; the Federal Reserve Bank of Chicago telephoned the Detroit Branch of the Federal Reserve Bank of Chicago; the Detroit Branch of the Federal Reserve Bank of Chicago telephoned the First National Bank of Detroit, and we went downstairs from our 16th floor offices to their vaults and obtained one hundred $1,000 bills.

When our policyholder called at our office with satchels and armed guards on each side of him, who were to escort him to the truck downstairs, he was mystified when we handed him a small envelope. With hands shaking, he opened it and looked as though he had just seen for the first time a $1,000 bill. He began to count, but was so nervous he only counted ninety-nine. After taking a few deep breaths, he started over again and finished with one hundred.

Within a few hours, the coal in the railroad yards had been released, trucks had started to travel in various directions through the city and countryside. Life insurance money had begun to "keep the home fires burning," to relieve suffering, make little children and elderly men and women warm, and prevent what could have been a very difficult health situation.

Two years prior to that memorable March of 1933, the coal dealer had decided, with some persuasion by our office, that he would be wise to set aside a considerable sum to guarantee the fulfillment of his financial plans for himself and family, regardless of what might happen to his business or his financial future in other respects. He purchased a $115,000 single premium endowment policy from us and, with this policy as security, the Company loaned him $100,000 and placed it in his hands within six hours after he had made a request for the loan.

In the election to the presidency of Bertrand J. Perry on the death of Mr. Sargeant, one more "career man" came to be the head of the Massachusetts Mutual. Mr. Perry had not begun with the Company while still a boy, as Mr. Sargeant had, but nearly all his business life had been spent in its employ. He also had risen by merit from one position to another. Born at Claremont, New Hampshire, on December 5, 1874, Mr. Perry had been brought by his parents, at the age of seven, to Springfield and was educated in the public schools. Like many another later captain of industry he peddled newspapers as a boy. He also added to the family income by lighting street lamps, then dependent on gas or kerosene. On graduating from high school he went with the Overman Wheel Company of Chicopee, whose Victor bicycles were, for a time, the highly profitable rage of the "Gay Nineties." But there came a slump in the bicycle business. After a brief trial of newspaper reporting, Mr. Perry joined the Massachusetts Mutual on June 7, 1897, as a clerk in the actuarial department. Five years later he was transferred to the premium record department and in 1912 he was made chief clerk and office manager. He was elected assistant secretary in 1915 and secretary in 1926. In January, 1928, he was elected vice president, made a member of the board of directors and placed in charge of the Company's investments. In January, 1936, a few days after the death of Mr. Sargeant, he was elected president.

It was written of Mr. Perry, at the time of his accession to the presidency, that he was one of the few insurance

Bertrand J. Perry, seventh president, 1936-1945.

officials who did not play golf. His other and greater distinctions were many. He had been one of the first to recognize the inadequacy of the Company's second Home Office building. He anticipated the need of larger quarters, laid plans for the efficient interior arrangement of the new building and, in 1924, was largely instrumental in the selection of its site. Assigned to the supervision of its construction, he worked in close co-operation with the architects and engineers. But he left his mark not only on the structure which housed the Company's operations. The mechanized efficiency of those operations, made possible by modern devices with mathematical brains, was largely due to his initiative in taking early advantage of the mechanical genius of the time.

While the first and heaviest impact of the depression fell on President Sargeant, it could be said that the difficult, many-sided task of clearing up after the storm fell upon President Perry. It was a task which especially related to the Company's investments. Not only were bonds, once regarded as gilt-edged, in default on their interest, but real estate, selected with the utmost care, had been thrown upon the Company's hands through the inability of the mortgagors to pay interest and, in some cases, to pay taxes. To nurse such properties back to the time and condition at which their fair value could be realized, and losses to the Company either minimized or prevented altogether, was an undertaking calling for sagacity, faith and patience. That Mr. Perry possessed these qualities in marked degree is evidenced by the successful manner in which these objectives were achieved. When Mr. Perry retired as president of the Company in 1945, he became chairman of the board of directors. But although he retired from that post, too, in June, 1948, the Company, as it approaches its centennial anniversary, still has the benefit, through his continuing service as a director, of the abilities which had made him an outstanding insurance executive.

On December 31, 1935, shortly before Mr. Perry became president, the Company's assets stood at $533,225,000 and its insurance in force at $1,851,447,000. On December 31, 1944, shortly before he retired as president and became chairman of the board, assets stood at $931,585,000 and insurance in force was $2,197,894,000. Thus under Mr. Perry the Company passed the milestone of two billion of insurance in force, as it had passed that of one billion under Mr. McClench.

Because mathematical computations play a peculiarly large part in the operations of a life insurance company, much history is condensed in the contrast between the elaborate mechanical equipment, with which those computations are made in the Home Office of the Massachusetts Mutual today, and the almost complete lack of such equipment at the Company's founding and for many years afterward.

The one man in the Company's history who would be most deeply impressed by all of these mechanical devices, if he could come back to life and watch them in operation while he toured the Company's present building, would be Francis B. Bacon, first secretary and once the Company's entire active force. As one studies the Company's first letter press volume with its faint tissue-paper reproductions of the letters Mr. Bacon wrote, in careful longhand, to prospective agents and policyholders, it is easy to imagine what might be his feelings if he were to limp about the marble-floored corridors of the Company's present offices.

Typical examples of electronic and mechanical equipment in daily use. (Above) The Electronic "Brain" performs all sorts of complicated calculations in the twinkling of an eye; (below) this machine prints vital data on a three-part Premium Notice form at the rate of forty complete forms a minute.

132

Mr. Bacon would surely linger in amazement as he watched noiseless typewriters, adding machines, calculators, addressing machines, tabulating machines, postage machines and dictating equipment. The latter, by the use of electronics, permits the recorded voice of the dictator either to be filed for future reference or to be played back to a stenographer for immediate typing. At first it would seem to him like witchcraft. But there could hardly fail to swell within him a sense of pride in having pioneered it all when he dipped his pen in the ink of 1851 and set things in motion as he wrote the Company's first letters. It was not until 1885 that the Company bought its first typewriter and sent out its first typewritten letter. That one typewriter belonged, so far as its operation was concerned, to President Edgerly's secretary—a mere man, since it was more than twenty years later that the first woman entered the employ of the Massachusetts Mutual in its Home Office.

Perhaps the most spectacular office equipment used by the Company is that which is classified as "punch card." Listed under that head are some forty-five different machines. This equipment operates on the basis of arithmetical or alphabetic information being recorded in small tabulating cards by a series of punched holes. By means of these punched holes the following operations may be performed at fantastic speeds and in a completely automatic fashion: 1. Sorting; the tabulating cards may be sorted into any one of twelve classifications at the rate of 650 cards per minute and by successive stages of sorting the cards may be placed in straight numerical order, may be grouped in predetermined classifications or may be sorted in straight alphabetical order. 2. Calculating machines; this equipment senses the numerical values punched in the tabulating cards

133

and performs complicated computations involving (in sequence) multiplications, divisions, subtractions, cross footings, combinations, pro-rating, etc., and does the complete job of computation in approximately one-thousandth of a second. The final answer is punched into the cards at the rate of one hundred completed cards per minute.

These machines depend upon electronic tubes for the calculations which they perform. The only moving parts involved are used in the punching of the answers into the respective cards. The equipment is similar, though on a smaller scale, to the larger so-called "electronic brains," recently publicized in connection with the Massachusetts Institute of Technology, Harvard University and the army and navy research programs. In addition to performing such calculations at almost incredible speed, these machines also check their own performance. If any part of a machine fails to function properly, so that a wrong answer would be produced, the machine stops and flashes a red light. This indicates which part of the machine is temporarily out of order. The whole process has been graphically described as "robot accounting."

The test of a battery of machine guns in war is the number of shots it can fire in a given time. The test of all these multiple batteries of business machines is the yearly total of transactions, necessary to the far-flung operations of the Massachusetts Mutual, which they make possible. Without these machines, operating for the most part noiselessly but always efficiently, a far larger clerical force would be necessary to serve the needs of more than half a million policyholders. And an even greater building would be necessary to house such an army of workers. The following tabulation shows some representative transactions handled at the

Home Office in a recent typical year. In most of these transactions business machines play an important part.

43,000 New policies issued.

560,000 Policy record cards prepared for Home Office
and agency use in connection with new policies
issued.

129,200 Policy servicing transactions, in connection
with policies already on the books, to meet
the current requirements of the policy owners.

61,000 Changes in policyholders' addresses recorded.

1,490,000 Premium and interest notices and receipts
sent to policyholders.

1,296,800 Premium collections recorded.

616,000 Dividend accumulation, loan, annuity and installment accounts (these accounts are com-
parable to bank accounts from a record keeping and servicing standpoint).

40,200 New loans made to policyholders.

21,000 Payments received and recorded on account
of loans to policyholders.

500,500 Checks issued to living policyholders and beneficiaries for cash dividends, dividend accumulations, loans, income payments, death benefits,
matured endowments, cash values, etc.

3,820,000 Pieces of incoming and outgoing mail handled.

The one-man Home Office force, represented by Mr.
Bacon in the beginning, became a sixteen-man force in
1884. Now that force is well on the way to being multiplied
by one hundred. Its size, together with the changes of the
time, invites its activities along many lines. When the present building was designed, a quarter century ago, provision

135

*The entrance rotunda of the present
Home Office building.*

was wisely made for some of these activities. The excellent auditorium and gymnasium provide facilities for a number of recreational and athletic diversions for the Home Office staff. Among these activities are basketball teams, softball teams, a glee club which presents annual Christmas and spring concerts and a dramatic club which usually gives two plays each year. One of the outstanding features of the Home Office building is its well-stocked and attractively arranged library. In addition to the large division of books having to do with life insurance, there is a generous provision of standard books of fiction and non-fiction. To a large degree the Company's building, with its cafeteria for luncheons, its banking facilities and its many other conveniences, is a well-appointed city in itself through the working hours of the day. In addition, it provides facilities for organized recreational activities in the evening.

With such a force backed by such an equipment, the Company's services, wholly outside the scope of life insurance, have followed naturally when there have been public emergencies to meet. One such opportunity for service came when, in the spring of 1936, a disastrous flood swept down the Connecticut River valley, disrupted travel and communication and drove thousands of people from their homes in low-lying sections which have since been protected by elaborate dikes. In this crisis the Massachusetts Mutual, secure on the high ground to the east of Springfield, served meals for many of those who were temporarily homeless.

The number of those driven from their homes in the immediate Springfield area was estimated at not less than 15,000. Some estimates put it as high as 20,000. The officers of the Massachusetts Mutual were alert to the proportions of the disaster. At an emergency conference held in President Perry's office March 20, 1936, it was decided to contact the local Red Cross immediately and to offer the Company's services. It was at once obvious that one of the major problems was that of feeding the refugees. Temporary shelter was provided for them in high schools, churches, the Y. M. C. A. buildings and other semi-public institutions. But in most cases these institutions lacked equipment for preparing meals.

It was promptly agreed that the Massachusetts Mutual should take over one of the five feeding centers which had been established and temporarily assume complete responsibility for it. The number of refugees expected at that center was first estimated by the Red Cross at 500. But the emergency grew so rapidly that, in spite of the large number of refugees who were fed in the homes of relatives and friends, no less than 1,100 were cared for at the first meal served by the Company. Throughout the most critical days the number served by the Company ran between 1,100 and 1,300 at each meal.

A far greater emergency came when the Nation was suddenly plunged into World War II by the Japanese attack at Pearl Harbor. Before that attack, however, a sense of impending crisis had led a selected group of employees to start in November, 1941, a Red Cross first aid instructors' course at the Home Office on their own time and initiative. The instructors so trained subsequently conducted many Company-sponsored classes at the office, as well as outside classes from the Red Cross. From this group came three chairmen of the Springfield Red Cross first aid committee. One of them later qualified as a water safety instructor and participated in water rescue instruction for the airmen

138

at the great Westover Air Base which was constructed near Springfield and is still maintained. The Company also received notable recognition for the part it was playing in the war effort when it was asked to lend eight instructors for first aid training of air force, pre-flight cadets at Springfield College.

Early in 1942 corridors on the first and second floors of the Home Office building were converted into air raid shelters by replacing all glass panels with heavy building board. First aid stations were equipped and frequent drills were held on signal throughout the building. The Company's auditorium was loaned to Civilian Defense organizations for various meetings. Some of the equipment of the medical division of Civilian Defense was stored in the building throughout the war. A colored movie of the work of the medical division was prepared for public showing. In this movie the Massachusetts Mutual Home Office building and the materials furnished by the Company, together with many of its employees, all had their part.

From January, 1941, through April, 1945, eighty-three men and twenty-eight women from the Home Office joined the armed services. When an employee left for military service, the Company paid a special military allowance of two to thirteen weeks pay, depending on length of service. Group insurance was continued on these employees as long as possible. When it could no longer be continued, the Company paid the premiums on equivalent amounts of National Service Life Insurance.

In all, 357 Massachusetts Mutual employees, including those from its agencies, donned the uniform for direct war service. Forty-six had been honorably discharged when the separate branches which they served and their number were given in August, 1945, in the *Listening Post*, the monthly periodical of "News about Our Men in the Armed Services" which was published by the Company, chiefly for their benefit. Of the remaining 311, the uniform of the Army had been worn by 191 including two WACS. Three had risen to be colonels, nine to be lieutenant colonels, nineteen to be majors, thirty-eight (including one of the WACS) to be captains and thirty-seven to be lieutenants.

In the Navy in World War II were eighty-eight from the Massachusetts Mutual, including nineteen WAVES. Three had risen to be lieutenant commanders; thirty-one (including one of the WAVES) to be lieutenants; ten (including two of the WAVES) to be lieutenants junior grade. In the Marine Corps there were eleven, one of whom became a major, and four lieutenants. In the Coast Guard there were ten (including four SPARS), two became lieutenants, and one lieutenant junior grade. One served in the Merchant Marine, ten in miscellaneous branches of the armed services. Of all these who wore their country's uniform, nine made the supreme sacrifice, seven being killed in action and two succumbing to disease.

When the government began to issue policies under the National Service Life Insurance Act of 1940, the Massachusetts Mutual strongly recommended their purchase. It formally took the position that it would not issue insurance to any member of the United States armed forces who was eligible for government life insurance, unless the applicant either already held or was applying for the full amount of such insurance which was available to him. Provision was also made so that Massachusetts Mutual policyholders in war service could settle their premiums on a monthly basis through deductions from their pay. Later on, through its field representatives, the Company distributed thousands of copies of the government booklet, "Continuance of National Service Life Insurance," to returning veterans. It also instructed its representatives to urge the veterans to continue this insurance and make it a part of their life insurance programs. The Company's Home Office employees and field representatives assisted materially in the sale of war bonds to individuals. The sales made by this loyal group, usually after regular working hours, aggregated many millions.

With World War II at an end, it was possible to review the Company's participation in the war effort as a completed whole. On December 31, 1945, having subscribed in increasing amounts to succeeding war loans, the Company owned and had on order United States government bonds with a par value of $286,000,000. The maximum amount of government bonds held by the Company during or shortly after the war period was $302,067,000 in September, 1946. That was the contribution in money. But as the Company's capacity for aid in that form had grown from a few thousands in the Civil War to hundreds of millions in World War II, so had the capacity of its personnel, both men and women, for patriotic service of many kinds.

To one of the Massachusetts Mutual's policyholders World War II brought a unique experience. Just before the Japanese landed in the Philippines she buried a steel box, containing her valuables, in her Manila garden. In it were her bonds, stocks, land titles and her policy in the Massachusetts Mutual. In February, 1945, when General MacArthur's forces reoccupied Manila, largely in ruins, the box was joyfully dug up. However, it had rusted through and the owner found her Massachusetts Mutual policy mildewed, rust-

141

marked and partially eaten away. She sent the damaged document to the Home Office, where it is still preserved, and received a new policy to replace it.

As the Company completes its first century one of the outstanding facts in regard to the Home Office force, which on July 1, 1950 numbered 1,332, is the large preponderance of women employees. Women in the Home Office outnumber men two to one, the figures on that date being 903 women to 429 men. It was not until 1909, however, that the first woman was employed by the Company. Since that time the number of women employees has not only greatly increased but many have been given important positions and several now serve in official capacities.

One of the pioneers in training Home Office personnel, the Company has a comprehensive educational program for both old and new employees. Through its Beginners School the new employee receives classroom instruction on the theory and fundamentals of life insurance. This formalized course, conducted by the personnel department, is supplemented by on-the-job training which is given the new employee before he is assigned to definite tasks. Special courses are also given, to qualify experienced employees for supervisory positions. Ample opportunities are offered all employees to improve their technical knowledge of the life insurance business through the well-organized and thorough courses provided by the Life Office Management Association. This is a national organization sponsored by the life insurance companies of the United States. Many Home Office employees are taking its courses while a considerable number have already received diplomas, and thirty-two have qualified as Associates and ten as Fellows.

Beginning with Oscar B. Ireland, who was a charter

142

member of the Actuarial Society of America at its founding in 1889, the actuarial personnel of the Company has been represented uninterruptedly in the membership of the professional bodies concerned with the study and advancement of actuarial science. When the Society of Actuaries was established in 1949 as the successor organization of the Actuarial Society of America and the American Institute of Actuaries (founded in 1909), six employees of the Company qualified as Fellows and five as Associates of the new organization. Admission to membership in the Society of Actuaries, as had been the case with its predecessors, requires the successful completion of a series of rigorous examinations. Employees in the Company's actuarial and group divisions who have adequate mathematical skills and training are encouraged to study for these examinations. Students have access to the Company's well-equipped actuarial library and are given assistance in their preparation for the examinations by making available to them courses of study in actuarial subjects.

For many years the Company has provided courses of supervised study and training for its field representatives. In 1950 this educational program was greatly broadened by the adoption of the new Massachusetts Mutual Training Program for Field Representatives which provides an education in the theory of life insurance and in its application to the solution of individualized insurance problems. This program extends over a period of two and one-half years and utilizes supervised training, class study, field work, and regional and Home Office schools. Representatives completing the course are trained in the handling of life insurance programs, business insurance, estate planning, tax phases of life insurance and pension trusts. Refresher courses on these subjects are given from time to time to qualified veteran representatives in order to keep them informed on new developments in these fields.

Many of the Company's representatives supplement the training they receive under its educational program by pursuing the comprehensive course offered by the American College of Life Underwriters. As of September, 1950, one hundred and twenty-three of them had received the Chartered Life Underwriter designation, awarded by the College upon successful completion of its study program and prescribed field experience requirements. Many others among the Company's representatives are engaging in this course of study which usually takes about four years.

As an indication of the caliber of the Company's field representatives, it is interesting to note that 267 of them received the 1950 National Quality Award, an annual recognition of meritorious service in the field of life underwriting sponsored by two national insurance organizations. Furthermore, fifty-two of them gained national prominence by attaining membership in the 1950 Million Dollar Round Table, a nationwide organization composed of life insurance agents selling $1,000,000 or more of insurance during a twelve-month period.

The Massachusetts Mutual's tower, a landmark on the main highway from Springfield to Boston.

CHAPTER VII

An End and a Beginning

On MAY 15, 1951, the hands of the big clock in the Massachusetts Mutual's tower, turning forward and not backward as any history must to find a starting point, will mark the end of one century of service and the beginning of another. The century that has ended has been marked by change and growth. But both change and growth have been the incidents of service. There seems no reason to suppose that, in this respect, the second century will be different.

The evolution of life insurance in one hundred years has been many-sided. The outstanding fact is that while the assets and insurance in force of the Massachusetts Mutual in 1951 have reached figures that would have seemed in-

145

credible in 1851, their growth has been the result, in part, of a similar multiplication of the forms of protection which the Company has offered. It is significant that the Company engaged solely, during its first fifty years, in the issuance of life insurance payable in a lump sum at death or maturity.

The turning point came in 1901, just a half century after the Company was founded. In that year, Mr. Hall being president, provision was first included in Massachusetts Mutual policies permitting their proceeds to be left with the Company and made payable in annual instalments, either for a fixed period or during the lifetime of the beneficiary. That increase of service, followed by many others during the fifty years from 1901, had two effects. It set in motion a new and continuing study of the many different needs which, in a highly organized and progressive economy, a life insurance company might properly serve. At the same time it determined, more definitely than before, a development which President Edgerly had resisted. This was the evolution of the life insurance business, through assumption of the custodial care of vast sums of money accumulated under policies of many forms, into the greatest of all investment trusts.

As the Massachusetts Mutual expanded and knowledge of life insurance became more general, the adaptation of life insurance to cover a wider variety of human needs was accelerated by the exploration of its agents into the problems of their individual clients. For example, cases would arise in which there was little need for additional insurance for the basic living requirements of the family but obvious need to provide a retirement income for the insured. From the study of such cases came the Company's first offer of single premium life annuities in 1917. At that time the

146

Company also offered an annual premium form, called a deferred annuity, under which the annuity payments began at attainment of the selected retirement age. In 1931, the annual premium deferred annuity was replaced by a retirement annuity which provided a wider choice of options available to the annuitant at maturity.

One of the human misfortunes limiting life insurance in the service it might render was that some form of disability might strike the policyholder and make him incapable of continuing the payment of his premiums. To prevent the lapse of policies through such causes the Massachusetts Mutual in 1914 first offered to attach to its policies, for a small extra premium, a clause which would provide for waiving premiums if the insured became totally and permanently disabled before attaining a specified age. But this did not replace the income which was lost by reason of disability. Policies were frequently surrendered, in order to obtain their cash value, when disability overtook their unfortunate holders. In 1918 the Company therefore broadened its service to furnish complete protection against disability. It then offered a clause which provided an income of $10.00 per month per $1,000 of insurance to the disabled policyholder, in addition to waiving his premiums.

Due to adverse experience during the depression in the early 1930's, most life insurance companies abandoned the income disability field entirely. They offered only a provision for the waiving of premium payments during disability. The Massachusetts Mutual, however, continued to offer income benefits but, in 1933, adopted a clause, for policies of current issue, providing an income of $5.00 per month per $1,000 of insurance. Experience under this more conservative income provision proved satisfactory. In 1950

147

the Company made an exhaustive review of its entire experience with the disability income feature. Feeling that there existed a real need for this type of insurance coverage in adequate amounts, especially on the part of young men who were bringing up families and who were entirely dependent upon their earned incomes, the Company again decided to offer a disability income benefit on the basis of $10.00 per month per $1,000 of insurance. This action was in line with the Company's constant endeavor to meet the public need for various types of insurance coverage.

In 1928 the Massachusetts Mutual first offered a provision calling for the payment of an additional death benefit equal to the sum insured in the event that death should be caused by accidental means. This provision proved very popular, largely because the extra premium required was so small when compared with the death benefit payable under such circumstances.

Among the more important of the Company's developments in new fields since 1937 have been those which come under the heads of pension trusts and group insurance. Here again evolution has been at work. The demonstrated needs of our present economy have led to the expansion of the Company's service to meet them. As the early copies of *The Radiator,* the Company's chief house organ, will show, there were those who, around 1913, thought little better of group insurance than President Edgerly had thought of the development of the life insurance business as the custodian of funds invested to yield continuing incomes to beneficiaries. Time marches on.

Following the enactment of the Social Security Act of 1937 many corporations desired to supplement the pensions which their employees would receive under that act by additional pensions to be purchased and paid for during the service of the employees. Few evidences of progress in social thinking and of the desire for broader protection have been so clear as the reception given by the public to various forms, now becoming more and more numerous, of group insurance. Under the stimulation of favorable tax laws and a growing interest on the part of both management and labor in long-range welfare and security plans, a marked trend toward the wholesale buying of insurance and pension benefits developed as early as 1941 and continued through the war years. In recognition of this trend the Massachusetts Mutual announced the organization of a group department, effective January 1, 1946. At that time the Home Office staff of the new department consisted of five persons and the field organization was merely a blueprint. Six months later an active field force had been created consisting of six regional managers, each responsible for group sales activities in a specified section of the country.

The increase in the personnel of the group department, in Home Office and field, to over 200 by July, 1950, is an index of the rapid expansion of its business. After four years of operation the wisdom of the Company's decision to enter the group field is indicated by the substantial volume of all lines of group insurance already placed in force.

As the Company's first century ends, one of the major issues is sharply defined by two opposing developments. On one side are those whose political philosophy inclines towards the constant expansion, in the field of insurance as well as in other fields, of governmental operations. On the other side is the demonstrated growth and broadening of the service rendered by the Massachusetts Mutual and other insurance companies. The question is of the vehicle to be used to provide social benefits—particularly hospital, surgical and medical care—and pensions for old age. The contribution of the Massachusetts Mutual to a wise public decision has been its own decision that group life insurance was not enough to meet the needs of the time or to fulfill its own determination to provide "the kind of insurance that is best fitted to meet postwar conditions." This has called for an extension of the Company's service into the group casualty field and the offering of a complete line of casualty contracts, including weekly disability, hospital, surgical, and medical expense insurance for employees and hospital and surgical expense insurance for dependents.

There is obvious significance, in connection with these developments, in the report of the Hoover Commission on the Reorganization of the Federal Government. That report has been especially severe in its condemnation of the inefficiency and wastefulness of the Veterans Administration, particularly its insurance activities. Such criticism is not of the service which is performed, but of the way in which it is performed, especially its delays. At the conference of the non-partisan Citizens Committee for the Hoover Report held in Washington in December, 1949, Thomas M. Searles, director of the task force which made an exhaustive study of the Veterans Administration and a veteran himself, declared: "The insurance problems in the Veterans Administration are extremely elementary, simple ones, as compared with the problems of the big insurance companies.

"Our investigation revealed," added Mr. Searles, "that the average commercial insurance company paid between 75 and 80 per cent of their death claims within fifteen days." Against this, Mr. Searles pointed out that in the primary business of the prompt settlement of death claims, so vitally

150

important to dependents, the Veterans Administration took approximately eighty days. Even allowing the Administration's claim that thirty-one of these days were due to the failure of the veterans' dependents to give the proper information, this left forty-nine days, or more than three times the average period required by the insurance companies for the settlement of the preponderant majority of their claims. Yet Mr. Searles also emphasized the fact that "the problems in settling a death claim in a private company are much more complicated than that for the Veterans Administration."

The Massachusetts Mutual's records for the year 1950 show that on the same day that *completed papers were received*, no less than 33 per cent of death claims were paid. By the second day, 77 per cent were paid, and by the third day, 93 per cent. Within four days following the receipt of completed papers, payment of practically 100 per cent of death claims had been made.

Finally, Mr. Searles declared that the detailed findings of his investigating force showed that: "on an average, the Veterans Administration employee in the insurance department does only one-fourth of the work done by the average employee in a commercial insurance company." In all this there was, it should be noted, no allegation of graft or dishonesty, but merely emphasis on the inefficiency and waste in the Veterans Administration as compared with the intelligent planning and economical operation which is found in the commercial companies, and which is fostered by the fact that they must compete with each other. The moral seems plain.

Two opposing factors which have vitally affected life insurance during the Massachusetts Mutual's hundred years have been the increasing length of the average life span and the decreasing return on invested funds. To a considerable degree the financial effects of these two factors have counter-balanced each other. Had either factor been absent, the effect of the other would necessarily have been to produce a marked change, either up or down, in the cost of life insurance.

Only meager data as to length of life in the United States are available for the nineteenth century as a whole. It is, therefore, impossible to say what the average length of life of residents of the United States was in 1851, when the Massachusetts Mutual was born, with the same accuracy with which such figures can be quoted near the end of the Company's first century. As has been shown, life insurance in its infancy in the United States depended largely on mortality tables which had been worked out in other countries. The expectancy of human life in England and Wales in 1841 was reported to be 40.19 years. At the end of the nineteenth century the average length of life in a representative area in the United States was forty-eight years for males and fifty-one years for females. This was held to represent a gain of perhaps fourteen years since 1800. But how greatly life expectancy at birth has increased in the United States since 1900, when the figure was 49.2 years, is shown by the fact that in 1949 it was estimated to be 67.2 years.

It would be impossible for the insurance companies to give an exact measure of their influence on such lengthening of the life span. But their influence has clearly been impor-tant. Any applicant who has determined that life insurance is desirable but who is rejected, after examination, comes under a new incentive. That incentive is to overcome the revealed defects, if correction is possible through medical care and wiser daily living. But, in common with other life insurance companies, the Massachusetts Mutual has done much more than this to focus attention on the problem of life extension. The life insurance companies have become a great clearing house of invaluable statistical information as to various diseases. They have been the allies of the medical profession, on which they so largely depend, and of the public health authorities.

One of the outstanding features of many successive Massachusetts Mutual annual reports has been their emphasis on the marked decrease in the percentage of deaths which have been caused by infectious diseases among policyholders. Dr. Howard B. Brown, who became medical director of the Massachusetts Mutual in 1949 on the retirement of Dr. Morton Snow, has furnished much of the following data concerning the Company's mortality experience. The progressive decrease in deaths due to tuberculosis has been especially notable. It is a fact, familiar even to laymen, that there have been marked advances in the treatment of tuberculosis. No longer does it ravage whole families as it did when it helped to fill the cemeteries throughout the Nation. The major reason for this reduction in mortality due to tuberculosis is the general improvement in sanitary conditions, as well as the early recognition and isolation of the infectious.

The Company's records show a similar progressive decrease in deaths from pneumonia. For many years pneumonia had exacted a heavy death toll. Then it followed tuberculosis in yielding place as a major cause of death. The reasons for this change were: first, the use of serums, then of sulfonamides and, more lately, of penicillin and allied

153

curative agents. These curative agents, now being multiplied and improved, have proven helpful with a majority of infectious troubles both general and specific.

Appeals to the public to subscribe funds for the study of diseases of the heart and of cancer emphasize, with the support of life insurance statistics, two causes of death which have been reflected in mounting figures. This increase has especially prompted the research conducted by the Life Insurance Medical Research Fund. This research is a joint effort, to which the Massachusetts Mutual and other life insurance companies contribute financially. It is supervised, however, by an independent group of scientists. -

Figures showing an increased percentage of deaths from cancer and heart disease are of great interest but, in some degree, may be misleading. One reason for the increase has been the fact that a larger percentage of lives has reached the older ages where such deaths are more common. Another very important reason is found in better and more accurate diagnoses. For example, years ago undoubtedly many deaths that were then presumed to be due to "acute indigestion" were actually deaths from heart disease; also many deaths that were actually from cancer were undoubtedly improperly classified.

The lengthening of life and the downward course of the interest rate also brought changes in the mathematical and legal bases of life insurance which had been enacted into the laws of the several states as a consequence of Elizur Wright's efforts when the Massachusetts Mutual was young. After the influenza epidemic which followed World War I, mortality experience underwent marked changes in extent and incidence. The conquest of many of the diseases of childhood and the advance made by medical science in the treatment of

154

all infectious diseases, resulted in a new pattern of death rates on a much lower scale. In fact in the 1930's and 40's the death losses incurred by the Massachusetts Mutual for all ages combined, consistently represented about 50% to 60% of the losses expected according to the American Experience Table of Mortality. (The saving, of course, constituted a most important element of the dividends paid by the Company.) This mortality table had been compiled shortly after the Civil War, and about 1900 had become one of the factors underlying the legal standard of solvency and equity for life insurance companies. While the continued use of the American Experience Table would not have affected policyholders prejudicially in any way, a sentiment in favor of replacing this antiquated mortality table found expression among many people conversant with life insurance and even among the general public.

The American Experience Table would inevitably have been superseded by a table reflecting more recent death rates, but the decline in the rate of interest earned on investments, which commenced with the onset of the depression, hastened the change. Lower interest earnings made compensating changes in premiums and reserves appropriate, and general action along this line for the industry as a whole was indicated in the thirties. World War II postponed a movement of this kind, but it was evident that it would probably take place as soon as conditions permitted.

With such prospects for an industry-wide change, the legislatures of practically all states, from 1945 to 1947, amended their insurance laws to require that all companies in their jurisdictions, not later than January 1, 1948, set up reserves and provide non-forfeiture benefits in newly issued policies, not less than those produced by using a new

155

Alexander T. Maclean, eighth president, 1945-1950.

mortality table. The new table, the Commissioners' Standard Ordinary Table of Mortality, was based on the mortality experienced by a number of United States companies in the period from 1930 to 1940. The earlier table, however, was retained as the standard for policies issued prior to the adoption of the new table. Most companies in conforming with these laws introduced lower interest rates for their calculations, more in harmony with investment prospects at the time. In the premiums and policy non-forfeiture values prepared by the Massachusetts Mutual as a result of this change in the insurance laws, it adopted the assumption of a minimum interest rate of $2\frac{1}{2}$ per cent per year in place of the 3 per cent rate which had been used for many years.

The change to the CSO basis (the widely used abbreviation for the full name) in the Massachusetts Mutual was made on October 16, 1947. The last prior change of this kind had taken place on October 1, 1907. However, the increase in the variety of types of insurance and annuity coverage offered, and in the complexity of policy provisions and Company practices which had developed in the forty-year interval, made the change a project of the most extensive sort. Under the direction of Harry H. Peirce, then vice president and actuary, the transition was made with no interruption in the normal operations of the Company. A whole series of new policy forms, with accompanying application blanks and other supplementary riders and documents, was prepared and printed. Premium rates for a wide array of plans of insurance were computed, as were the cash surrender values and the non-forfeiture benefits provided under the Company's policies and the reserves which the insurance laws of the several states required to be maintained. In addition, two forms of rate manual were designed

157

and printed and new record forms were installed throughout the Company for efficient handling of the new class of policies.

One important phase in the evolution of the Massachusetts Mutual's policies and the broadening of its service to the public has been its acceptance of what are known as substandard risks. This means the issuance of insurance to men and women whose chances of living a normal number of years are reduced through some physical impairment, adverse family history, or engaging in a hazardous occupation. The experience of many years has enabled these risks to be classified and a proper extra premium charged to offset the additional hazard involved. An obviously expanded economic and social service is performed by the life insurance companies when they insure the greatest possible percentage of applicants. Those who are substandard risks are in greater danger of early death than people of normal life expectancy and, consequently, are fortunate to be able to obtain life insurance. The broadening of the service offered by the Massachusetts Mutual in this highly important field may be measured by the fact that since 1937 the Company has been in a position to insure substandard risks whose death rate is as much as five times the normal average.

Such broadening of the Company's service through the multiplication of the forms of protection it offers has been a development especially of its second half century. It is also significant that much of this development came after Alexander T. Maclean joined the Company as assistant actuary in 1916, and that the process was accelerated to a marked degree when he became president in 1945. Like Presidents Edgerly, Hall, Sargeant and Perry before him, Mr. Maclean, when he became president, had been a

158

"career man." There was, however, a distinction between the degree in which that description applied to them and in which it applied to him. All had grown up in the insurance business. But Mr. Maclean, unlike any of his predecessors, had, of his own choice, before joining the ranks of active insurance workers, enjoyed the benefits of a formal education designed to fit him for such service. He was a "career man" with that initial advantage. He was also the first actuary to become president of the Massachusetts Mutual, although actuaries had headed numerous other important insurance companies.

Mr. Maclean was born in Glasgow, Scotland, July 8, 1887. He was educated in the Glasgow schools and took special courses at Glasgow University, where he concentrated on mathematics. He then determined to pursue further studies in Edinburgh which would prepare him for the degree of Fellow of the Faculty of Actuaries. His training in this specialized line was under the direction of William A. Robertson, actuary of the Century Insurance Company of Edinburgh.

The Clan Maclean was an ancient clan, its history intertwined far back with the history of Scotland. The transfer of the Clan, so far as it was represented by Alexander T., to this country took place in 1910. Before that, having completed his training under "Willie" Robertson, he had worked for about three years in the actuarial department of the City of Glasgow Life Assurance Company. With him in that department were men who have since made their mark in the insurance world both in this country and in Great Britain.

On arriving in New York in November, 1910, Mr. Maclean immediately obtained a position with the Home Life

159

Insurance Company on applying to Henry Moir, a fellow Scot, then actuary and vice president. In 1916, just as Mr. Maclean was about to start on a honeymoon trip to Canada, Charles H. Angell, then actuary of the Massachusetts Mutual, asked him to come to Springfield as assistant actuary. The honeymoon was delayed while Mr. Maclean made a trip to Springfield to look the ground over. Shortly afterward Mr. Maclean began the service with the Massachusetts Mutual which was to lead to his election as president. In 1922 he was made associate actuary and in 1927, on the death of Mr. Angell, he was elected actuary. In 1929 he was made a director of the Company. The service which had been marked by these and other advancements, including his election as vice president in 1936, culminated in his election as president in 1945. But his conspicuous and invaluable service was cut short by death on May 15, 1950, just ninety-nine years to a day after the Company's founding.

The striking financial results which were achieved by the Massachusetts Mutual during Mr. Maclean's service as president are emphasized by figures which closely correspond as to dates with the beginning and the end of that service. On December 31, 1944, shortly before his election, the Company's assets stood at $931,585,000 and insurance in force was $2,197,894,000. On May 1, 1950, only a few days before Mr. Maclean's death, assets had risen to $1,343,000,000 and insurance in force had risen to $3,009,808,000.

On May 19, 1950, when the Company had progressed four days into its hundredth year, Vice President Leland J. Kalmbach was elected as its ninth president, to take on the responsibilities which had fallen from Mr. Maclean's shoulders. To Mr. Kalmbach, who had been born in Chelsea, Michigan, April 30, 1901, went the initial distinction of being, at forty-nine years of age, the youngest president the Massachusetts Mutual had yet had. In spite of that fact, which held out the promise of a longer term of service than was possible for any of his three immediate predecessors, Mr. Kalmbach had already achieved notable distinction in the insurance world. Educated in the public schools of Chelsea and at the University of Michigan, he had graduated at the latter with high honors, gaining the Phi Beta Kappa key by his rank as a scholar. He had majored in business administration and actuarial mathematics, thus laying the professional foundation, as Mr. Maclean had at Glasgow, for a life insurance career.

In 1924 Mr. Kalmbach joined the actuarial department of the Lincoln National Life Insurance Company of Fort Wayne, Indiana. He served that company for twenty-three years, receiving numerous promotions and becoming one of the country's best known actuaries and life insurance officers. One of his chief activities in his work with the Lincoln National was the expansion of the reinsurance operations of that company. In carrying on this activity he visited most of the leading life insurance companies of the country. His first contact with the Massachusetts Mutual was in connection with negotiations through which a reinsurance contract between these two companies was effected in 1937. During the ensuing years of frequent association with the officers of the Massachusetts Mutual, he gained their high professional respect and personal goodwill. It was, therefore, natural that when the officers and directors of the Company felt it advisable to add an experienced insurance executive to its official family, Mr. Kalmbach's name should have come to their minds.

Leland J. Kalmbach, ninth president, 1950-

Mr. Kalmbach was first vice president and a director of the Lincoln National Life Insurance Company when he resigned to join the Massachusetts Mutual as vice president on January 1, 1948, being elected a director the following month. As a member of the finance committee, agency committee and committee on death claims, he promptly assumed large responsibilities in the management of the Company and rapidly gained a wide experience in its operations. Under his direction the underwriting practices of the Massachusetts Mutual were further liberalized and other changes made which resulted in improved service to policyholders and greater co-operation with the Company's field representatives. He is, in fact, regarded as a field-minded company officer, commanding the friendly respect and devotion of the general agents and agents, his fellow officers and the Home Office personnel.

Among former officials of the Company whose faithful service contributed substantially to its progress and success, certain ones are especially remembered by their contemporaries and successors. Their full terms of service to the Company are indicated in parentheses in the following résumé. Wheeler H. Hall (40 years) served as secretary from 1908 until his death in 1926. Arthur K. McGinley (17 years) was appointed counsel in 1909 and served in that capacity until he died in 1920. Charles H. Angell (29 years) served as actuary from 1914 until his death in 1927. Dr. Morton Snow (47 years) served as medical director from 1917 until his retirement in 1948. Frank G. Hodskins (8 years) served as counsel from 1920 until his death in 1928. Henry Loeb (47 years) served as vice president from 1928 until his death in 1942. Samuel J. Johnson (48 years) served as secretary from 1928 until his retirement in 1950. Wesley

E. Monk (19 years) served as general counsel from 1929 until his retirement in 1947. William A. Rawlings (48 years) served as vice president from 1936 until his retirement in 1940. Joseph C. Behan (52 years) served as vice president from 1936 until his retirement in 1948. Albert D. Shaw (45 years) elected vice president in 1948, retired in 1949. In the appendix will be found a roster of all senior officials who have served the Company during its first one hundred years, as well as a list of its executive officers as of February 1, 1951.

A vital element in the growth of the Massachusetts Mutual, from its modest beginnings to its present striking proportions, has been its agency force. Spreading from a handful of field representatives in a single state in 1851, the year 1951 finds the Company with eighty-seven general agencies and 110 district agency offices in forty-three states and the District of Columbia, manned by ninety-six general agents and over 1,000 full-time field representatives. Since experience, as well as training, is an important element in developing the ability and efficiency of field personnel, it is worthy of note that nearly one-half of these general agents and field representatives have been with the Company for over five years; 39 per cent for over ten years; 32 per cent for over fifteen years; and 21 per cent for over twenty years. One hundred and eighty of these faithful representatives have served the Company for more than twenty-five years. Through the years these men and women, and their predecessors, have spread the mantle of Massachusetts Mutual protection over hundreds of thousands of American families. Many of them have been, as many of them are today, leaders not only in life insurance circles, but also in civic and religious activities in their communities. Salesmanship,

164

the art of introducing and distributing useful products and services, has been an important factor in bringing to American families many creature comforts and a high degree of financial security. Recognition is due to the past and present generations of Massachusetts Mutual salesmen. They have contributed their full share towards the establishment and maintenance in the United States of the highest standard of living the world has yet known.

Like every other phase of the life insurance business, that concerned with the investment of funds, which is vital to the performance of its entire service, has gone through a process of evolution. In this case the process has become more notable and has attracted more public attention because the sums calling for investment have grown so great. This has involved an increasing recognition, especially on the part of the large insurance companies, of their responsibilities in the preservation of our free economy.

Bonds and mortgages have been the traditional form of investment for insurance funds. This policy stems, in part, from the theory that, having future claims to meet for a certain number of dollars, life insurance companies should have their assets invested in securities which call for fixed interest payments and have fixed maturity dates, rather than in securities whose dividend payments are optional with the management. Security rather than high return has been the yardstick. This traditional policy was firmly established, so far as the Massachusetts Mutual was concerned, long before the Armstrong-Hughes investigation of 1906, with its disclosures of stock manipulation, gave it wider application. In recent years, however, it became clear that many of the best and strongest corporations in the country were opposed to having any bonded debt outstanding. To have

165

*At Rockefeller Center, New York—twenty-six-story office building
erected by the Company as an investment, 1950-1951.*

166

any share in the financial strength which these companies represented it was therefore necessary to invest in their common or preferred stocks. This, coupled with the fact that interest rates on good bonds were unusually low and that an adequate volume of sound mortgages was difficult to secure, resulted in the Company's decision to invest a moderate percentage of its funds in stocks. The Company has, however, adopted the conservative practice of applying a portion of the dividends received each year on both common and preferred stocks to a reduction of their book values.

The Company's ownership of real estate—other than the Home Office building—is another result of the growing scarcity of good fixed interest investments. Until 1947, life insurance companies were prohibited by the insurance laws of most states from purchasing real estate, except for use by the companies themselves. That is to say, real estate could not be bought for investment. Under these laws, even real estate acquired through foreclosure of mortgage loans had to be sold within a limited period, unless specific permission to hold it was granted by the state insurance commissioner having jurisdiction. Following the depression of the 1930's, several insurance companies in New York State requested the Legislature to consider an amendment to the law which would permit the life insurance companies to own a modest amount of real estate for investment purposes. As a consequence, legislation was passed permitting life insurance companies domiciled in New York to invest not more than 3 per cent of their assets in income-producing real estate. Later on other states followed suit, including Massachusetts.

The present most striking illustration of the Company's

168

*irview of Company's Home Office building showing recently
mpleted extensions of east and west wings of main building,
and enlargement of warehouse structure in rear.*

169

policy with regard to real estate investment is the twenty-six-story office building which it has erected in 1950-51 on a site adjoining Rockefeller Center at 600 Fifth Avenue in New York City. Since this particular area represents what is perhaps the most highly desired business location in the metropolis, the Company anticipates, as the building is completed and its occupancy is begun, a very satisfactory return on this investment.

In no other century than that now completed during the life of the Massachusetts Mutual have men been exposed to so many new ideas of their own making or to the discovery of so many new facts of Nature's making. Some of the new ideas have proved sound; some have proved false. As to others, the debate still continues; the proof hangs in the balance. As for the facts, once they are established they cannot be disputed. Yet, like the facts of nuclear fission, they can be very difficult to deal with. What, at the beginning of the Company's first century, seemed a rapidly changing world seems now, in retrospect, a world that was almost standing still; a world that, if one could, it might be pleasant to move back to—except that there would be frequent inconveniences to which it might not be easy to adjust.

The experience of the past hundred years emphasizes the soundness of the idea, the validity of the factual basis, on which life insurance companies, the Massachusetts Mutual outstanding among them, were founded. For that idea, the idea of protecting one's own and safeguarding one's future, implemented by the facts embodied in mortality tables and by the operation of compound interest, has helped to bring order into economic existence and to resolve doubts, so far as economic doubts can be resolved, for the individual human being and his family. His freedom, and the economic

170

stability which makes it possible for him to enjoy freedom, are the basis of our civilization—a civilization worth keeping at any sacrifice that it may cost.

As the Massachusetts Mutual passes its one hundredth milestone, the following message from President Kalmbach, the man who will lead the Company into its second century of progress, is an appropriate close to this hundred year history.

"As we review the record of the Massachusetts Mutual during the past one hundred years, we realize how proud the founders of the Company would be if they could see the result of their vision and humble effort. In their day and age, it was doubtless inconceivable that any life insurance company would ever attain the size to which their Company has grown.

"We salute those who have preceded us, for their part in building the Massachusetts Mutual to its present stature as one of the country's largest and strongest life insurance companies. We respect their integrity, which has been evidenced by the high order of trusteeship that has existed in their management of the affairs of the Company. We respect their wisdom in formulating such sound principles of operation—principles which have been followed continuously to this day and which have earned and preserved the Company's proud reputation for being a policyholders' company.

"The members of the present managerial staff of the Company are imbued with the same strong sense of trusteeship that has guided our predecessors. We dedicate ourselves to the diligent performance of the duties entrusted to us; and we pledge ourselves to be governed always by the best interests of our policyholders, to the end that the Com-

171

pany may furnish safe and broad insurance protection at the lowest possible cost for the character of service rendered.

"In thinking of the future, there is a feeling of real satisfaction in knowing that the institution of life insurance will continue to make a most important contribution to the very existence of the American way of life. It plays a vital role in the economic life of our Nation in acting as a reservoir for small savings of millions of the country's citizens and in making these funds available for financing the needs of industry, of home ownership, and of governmental bodies. Also, there is no factor in our economy which makes a greater contribution to the spirit of self-reliance and personal independence than does the institution of life insurance, which furnishes the only sure means by which millions of men can provide for their dependents and for their own financial security. It is inconceivable that ideologies like Communism could ever become a real threat in a nation of life insurance owners.

"As we stand upon the threshold of our second century of service, we face the future with faith and confidence and with the firm determination that the Massachusetts Mutual shall always be a strong force in the continuing economic and moral growth of our great Nation."

DIRECTORS
MASSACHUSETTS MUTUAL LIFE INSURANCE COMPANY
FEBRUARY 1, 1951

JOHN M. COLLINS
Springfield, Mass.
President, Moore Drop Forging Co.

CHESTER O. FISCHER
Vice President

RICHARD C. GUEST
Vice President

P. D. HOUSTON
Nashville, Tenn.
*Honorary Chairman of the Board,
The American National Bank*

LELAND J. KALMBACH
President

RICHMOND LEWIS
Springfield, Mass.
*President,
The Charles C. Lewis Co.*

173

DIRECTORS
(continued)

HAROLD A. LEY
Melvin Village, N. H.
Director,
Bush Terminal Buildings Co.

R. DeWITT MALLARY
Springfield, Mass.
Attorney at Law,
Mallary and Gilbert

CHARLES C. McELWAIN
Springfield, Mass.
President,
Mutual Fire Assurance Co.

JOSEPH K. MILLIKEN
North Dighton, Mass.
Treasurer,
Mount Hope Finishing Co.

GILBERT H. MONTAGUE
New York, N. Y.
Attorney at Law

WILLIAM H. NYE
Boston, Mass.
Vice President,
Turner Construction Co.

HARRY H. PEIRCE
Vice President

174

DIRECTORS
(*continued*)

BERTRAND J. PERRY
Norwich, Vermont
Former Chairman of the Board

CHARLES F. ROBBINS
New York, N. Y.
President,
A. G. Spalding & Bros., Inc.

G. VICTOR SAMMET
Boston, Mass.
resident, Northern Industrial
Chemical Co.

E. KENT SWIFT
Whitinsville, Mass.
Chairman of the Board,
Whitin Machine Works

EDWARD H. THOMSON
Springfield, Mass.
Director, Springfield Fire and
Marine Ins. Co.

ANDREW B. WALLACE
Springfield, Mass.
President,
Forbes & Wallace, Inc.

HAROLD J. WALTER
Uxbridge, Mass.
President, Bachmann Uxbridge
Worsted Corporation

175

*Interior Court of Home Office building
gay with the colorful blossoms of spring.*

176

APPENDIX

SENIOR OFFICIALS

OF THE

MASSACHUSETTS MUTUAL LIFE INSURANCE COMPANY

1851-1951

Chairmen of the Board

WILLIAM W. McCLENCH..1928-1928
BERTRAND J. PERRY 1945-1948

Presidents

CALEB RICE 1851-1873
EPHRAIM W. BOND 1873-1886
MARTIN V. B. EDGERLY..1886-1895
JOHN A. HALL 1895-1908
WILLIAM W. McCLENCH..1908-1928
WILLIAM H. SARGEANT ...1928-1936
BERTRAND J. PERRY 1936-1945
ALEXANDER T. MACLEAN.1945-1950
LELAND J. KALMBACH....1950-

Vice Presidents

JAMES M. THOMPSON.....1851-1851
ERASMUS D. BEACH 1851-1867
EPHRAIM W. BOND 1867-1873
CHARLES M. KNOX 1873-1874
HENRY FULLER, JR. 1874-1885
MARTIN V. B. EDGERLY
    Second Vice President 1883-1885
    Vice President 1885-1886
HENRY S. LEE 1886-1902
JULIUS H. APPLETON 1902-1904
HENRY M. PHILLIPS 1904-1909
WILLIAM W. McCLENCH
    Second Vice President 1905-1908
WILLIAM H. SARGEANT
    Second Vice President 1908-1909
    Vice President 1909-1928

Vice Presidents (continued)

OSCAR B. IRELAND
    Second Vice President 1909-1914
HENRY LOEB
    Second Vice President 1914-1928
    Vice President 1928-1942
CHARLES H. ANGELL
    Third Vice President 1926-1927
BERTRAND J. PERRY 1928-1936
OSGOOD E. FIFIELD
    Second Vice President 1928-1932
ALEXANDER T. MACLEAN
    Second Vice President 1928-1936
    Vice President 1936-1945
JOSEPH C. BEHAN
    Second Vice President 1928-1936
    Vice President 1936-1948
WILLIAM A. RAWLINGS
    Second Vice President 1933-1936
    Vice President 1936-1940
CHESTER O. FISCHER 1936-
HARRY H. PEIRCE 1944-
ALBERT D. SHAW
    Second Vice President 1944-1948
    Vice President 1948-1949
H. S. PAYSON ROWE
    Second Vice President 1944-1945
RALPH R. COOMBS
    Second Vice President 1944-1948
    Vice President 1948-
HOMER N. CHAPIN
    Second Vice President 1945-1948
    Vice President 1948-

Vice Presidents (continued)

LELAND J. KALMBACH 1948-1950
J. TRUMAN STRENG
   Second Vice President 1948-1951
   Vice President 1951-
RICHARD C. GUEST 1950-
CHARLES H. SCHAAFF 1950-
WRAYBURN M. BENTON
   Second Vice President 1950-
MICHAEL MARCHESE
   Second Vice President 1951-

Secretaries

FRANCIS B. BACON 1851-1870
CHARLES M. KNOX 1870-1873
AVERY J. SMITH 1873-1881
JOHN A. HALL 1881-1895
HENRY M. PHILLIPS 1895-1904
WILLIAM H. SARGEANT ... 1905-1908
WHEELER H. HALL 1908-1926
BERTRAND J. PERRY 1926-1928
SAMUEL J. JOHNSON 1928-1950
HARRISON B. CLAPP 1951-

Treasurers

CALEB RICE 1851-1873
EPHRAIM W. BOND 1873-1886
LEWIS J. POWERS 1886-1887

From 1887 to 1926 the duties of Treasurer were performed by the Secretary ... from 1926 on by the Financial Secretary.

Financial Secretaries

WHEELER H. HALL 1926-1926
ALBERT D. SHAW 1928-1948
RAYMOND M. COLTON ... 1948-

Actuaries

JAMES WEIR MASON 1870-1872
OSCAR B. IRELAND 1872-1914
CHARLES H. ANGELL 1914-1927
ALEXANDER T. MACLEAN . 1927-1936
HARRY H. PEIRCE 1936-1951
LOUIS LEVINSON 1951-

Medical Directors

DR. ALFRED LAMBERT ... 1851-1868
DR. DAVID P. SMITH 1868-1881
DR. ALFRED LAMBERT ... 1881-1885
DR. FREDERICK W. CHAPIN 1885-1911
DR. GEORGE S. STEBBINS .. 1911-1917
DR. MORTON SNOW 1917-1948
DR. HOWARD B. BROWN .. 1949-

General Counsels

GIDEON WELLS 1886-1895
WILLIAM W. McCLENCH . 1895-1908
ARTHUR K. McGINLEY ... 1909-1920
FRANK G. HODSKINS 1920-1928
WESLEY E. MONK 1929-1947
JOHN F. HANDY 1948-

EXECUTIVE OFFICERS

OF THE

MASSACHUSETTS MUTUAL LIFE INSURANCE COMPANY

FEBRUARY 1, 1951

LELAND J. KALMBACH, *President*

HARRY H. PEIRCE
Vice President

LOUIS LEVINSON
Actuary

CHESTER O. FISCHER
Vice President

RAYMOND M. COLTON
Financial Secretary

RICHARD C. GUEST
Vice President

HARRISON B. CLAPP
Secretary

RALPH R. COOMBS
Vice President

HOWARD B. BROWN, M.D.
Medical Director

HOMER N. CHAPIN
Vice President

RICHARD LITTLE
Associate Actuary

CHARLES H. SCHAAFF
Vice President

WALTER C. SULLIVAN
Associate Counsel

J. TRUMAN STRENG
Vice President

ROWLAND H. LONG
Associate Counsel

WRAYBURN M. BENTON
Second Vice President

CHARLES G. HILL
Group Secretary

MICHAEL MARCHESE
*Second Vice President
and Underwriting Secretary*

JOHN R. SIMPSON, JR.
Investment Secretary

JOHN F. HANDY
General Counsel

WILLIAM R. CHRISTMAS
Group Actuary

THOMAS S. SEXTON, M.D.
Associate Medical Director

THE ORIGINAL SUBSCRIBERS WHO MADE THE
MASSACHUSETTS MUTUAL POSSIBLE

We, the undersigned, agree to take the number of shares placed against each of our respective names of the Capital Stock of the Massachusetts Mutual Life Insurance Company chartered in Massachusetts, May 15, A. D. eighteen hundred and fifty-one.

SHARES, ONE HUNDRED DOLLARS EACH

Subscriber	Number of Shares
PHILOS B. TYLER	50
RUFUS CHANDLER	20
ALFRED LAMBERT	40
HARVEY DANKS	20
WAITSTILL HASTINGS	50
WM. W. BOYINGTON	20
ALEXANDER H. AVERY	50
EDMUND FREEMAN	50
WILLIAM RICE	50
HENRY FULLER, JR.	50
JOHN HAMILTON	25
CHARLES PHELPS	25
JAMES P. CHAPMAN	20
GEO. W. RICE	25
ABEL D. CHAPIN	50
J. O. MOSELEY	25
GEORGE MERRIAM	50
SAMUEL S. DAY	50
DANIEL COLLINS	20
WM. W. LEE	20
WILLIAM E. RICE	10
C. F. COLLINS	10
W. B. CALHOUN	15
S. L. DICKERMAN	15
HARVEY WOLCOTT	15
CALEB RICE	25
E. F. MOSELEY	25
R. A. CHAPMAN	25
HENRY GRAY	50
E. D. BEACH	50
GEO. DWIGHT	50

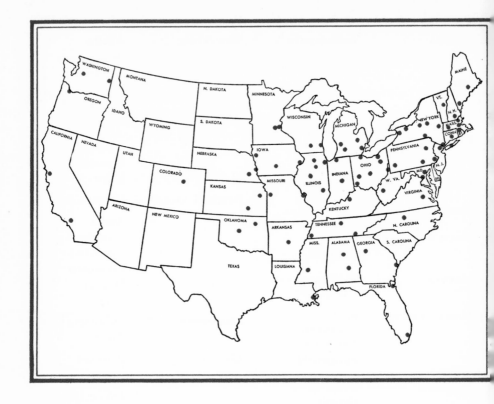

Nationwide Service

The Massachusetts Mutual has eighty-seven general agencies and twenty-one group offices in eighty cities, as well as 110 district agencies at other points in the United States. The above map shows the location of the cities where general agency and group offices are maintained. They are listed below in alphabetical order by States.

ALABAMA	Birmingham Montgomery	FLORIDA	Jacksonville Miami
ARKANSAS	Little Rock	GEORGIA	Atlanta Savannah
CALIFORNIA	Los Angeles San Francisco	ILLINOIS	Chicago (2 offices)
COLORADO	Denver		La Salle
CONNECTICUT	Hartford		Mattoon Peoria
DIST. OF COLUMBIA	Washington		Rockford

182

INDIANA	Indianapolis	NEW YORK	Albany
	South Bend		Binghamton
			Brooklyn
IOWA	Davenport		Buffalo
	Des Moines		Hempstead
	Sioux City		New York
			(3 offices)
KANSAS	Topeka		Rochester
	Wichita		Syracuse
			Utica
KENTUCKY	Louisville		
		NORTH CAROLINA	Greensboro
LOUISIANA	New Orleans	OHIO	Akron
MAINE	Bangor		Cincinnati
	Portland		Cleveland
			Columbus
MARYLAND	Baltimore		Dayton
	(2 offices)		Toledo
MASSACHUSETTS	Boston	OKLAHOMA	Oklahoma City
	(2 offices)		Tulsa
	Lawrence		
	Springfield	OREGON	Portland
MICHIGAN	Battle Creek	PENNSYLVANIA	Harrisburg
	Detroit		Philadelphia
	Flint		Pittsburgh
	Grand Rapids		Wilkes-Barre
		RHODE ISLAND	Providence
MINNESOTA	Minneapolis	TENNESSEE	Chattanooga
	St. Paul		Memphis
MISSISSIPPI	Jackson		Nashville
MISSOURI	Kansas City	VERMONT	Barre
	St. Louis	VIRGINIA	Richmond
	(2 offices)		
		WASHINGTON	Seattle
NEBRASKA	Lincoln		Spokane
	Omaha	WEST VIRGINIA	Charleston
NEW HAMPSHIRE	Manchester		Wheeling
NEW JERSEY	Newark	WISCONSIN	Madison
	(2 offices)		Milwaukee

MASSACHUSETTS MUTUAL
MILESTONES

1851 May 15, Company's charter granted by Commonwealth of Massachusetts, following subscription by thirty-one citizens of Springfield to guarantee capital stock of $100,000 in accordance with the charter.

First meeting of stockholders held and twenty directors chosen. Directors lease one-room office in Foot's Block, corner of State and Main Streets, Springfield, Massachusetts. This room is Home Office of Company for sixteen years.

Caleb Rice elected president and Francis B. Bacon, secretary.

August 2, Company issues its first policy insuring life of Harvey Danks, amount $1200.

1852 Caleb Rice, president of Company, elected first mayor of Springfield.

March 1, first death claim paid, amount $1000.

Agents appointed in New Haven, Conn.; Providence, R. I.; Nashua, N. H.; Portland, Maine; Worcester, Lowell, East Bridgewater, Beverly and Middleboro, Mass.

July 31, end of first year of operation, insurance in force 341 policies for $370,495.

1853 July 31, end of second year of operation, insurance in force 422 policies for $547,895.

1855 Insurance in force passes $1,000,000. Agencies established in New York City, Chicago, Cleveland, Detroit and Albany.

1856 Death of George W. Rice, leader in founding of Company.

1858 First cash values paid on surrendered policies.

First endowment policy issued.

1859 First mortgage loan made, amount $2000.

1861 The first Non-Forfeiture law, the Massachusetts law requiring the granting of extended insurance on lapsed policies, becomes effective.

First dividend paid to policyholders.

1864 Insurance in force passes $10,000,000.

1865 Assets pass $1,000,000.

1866 December, cornerstone laid for Company's first Home Office building at 413 Main Street, Springfield, Massachusetts.

1867 September 9, policyholders vote to retire capital stock of $100,000, and subscribers are repaid.

1868 First Home Office building occupied.

1869 Free permits granted to policyholders to travel and reside west of Rocky Mountains.

Company's fiscal year changed from year ending July 31, to year ending December 31.

1873 February 5, Home Office building gutted by fire.

March 1, death of Caleb Rice, president 1851-1873.

March 4, Vice President Ephraim W. Bond elected president.

December 10, restored Home Office building reoccupied.

1880 New Non-Forfeiture law, requiring the granting of paid-up insurance on lapsed policies, enacted by Massachusetts Legislature.

1884 Home Office staff consists of three officers and thirteen clerks.

1886 February 2, President Ephraim W. Bond declines re-election and Vice President Martin Van Buren Edgerly elected president.

1889 Assets pass $10,000,000, insurance in force passes $50,000,000.

1891 December 5, death of Ephraim W. Bond, president 1873-1886.

1895 March 18, death of Martin Van Buren Edgerly, president 1886-1895.

March 28, Secretary John A. Hall elected president.

1896 Insurance in force passes $100,000,000.

1901 Adoption of American Experience Mortality Table and 3½% interest as basis for premium rates and reserves, in place of Actuaries' Table and 4% interest formerly used.

1904 First policy with Installment Options provisions issued.

1907 Home Office staff numbers 100.

October 1, adoption of American Experience Mortality Table and 3% interest as basis for premium rates and reserves.

1908 Revised Massachusetts Non-Forfeiture law becomes effective, providing for automatic paid-up insurance and alternative extended term insurance or cash surrender value.

September 3, death of John A. Hall, president 1895-1908.

October 9, occupation of Company's second Home Office building on the site of Foot's Block where first one-room office was located.

October 28, Second Vice President and General Counsel William W. McClench elected president.

Assets pass $50,000,000.

1910 Privilege given policyholders of applying dividend credits to make policies paid-up in full or to mature them as endowments.

1911 July 1, adoption of Automatic Premium Loan provision.

1914 January 1, adoption of Waiver of Premium provision covering disability occurring before age 60.

1917 First annuity issued.

Assets pass $100,000,000.

1918 May 1, adoption of clause providing for waiver of premium and for income (at first $100 per year, later $10 per month, per $1000 of insurance) in event of disability occurring before age 60.

1919 Adoption of program of Group Insurance, placed in other companies, for Home Office and Field personnel.

Carbon copies of letters supersede tissue copies laboriously made on letter presses prior to this time.

Insurance in force passes $500,000,000.

1923 January 1, adoption of liberal provision permitting reinstatement of policies *within thirty-one days after expiration of grace period* on application by insured, and *without evidence of insurability.*

Insurance in force passes one billion dollars.

1926 Policies in connection with Salary Savings Plans first issued.

Company begins to insure applicants from ten years of age (former minimum age, 14).

1927 July, Company occupies present Home Office building at 1295 State Street, Springfield, Massachusetts.

1928 January 25, William W. McClench, president 1908-1928, elected chairman of the board and Vice President William H. Sargeant elected president.

Adoption of Accidental Death Benefit provision.

November 16, death of Chairman of Board William W. McClench.

1930 First Family Income policy issued.

Insurance in force passes two billion dollars.

1933 February 1, disability riders revised, and disability income benefit limited to $5 per $1000 of insurance.

1934 First Family Maintenance policy issued.

June 23, President Sargeant completes fifty years with Company. Field force marks day with 6600 applications for over $29,000,000 of new insurance.

1935 New training course for agents, "Massachusetts Mutual Selling," adopted.

December 28, death of William H. Sargeant, president 1928-1936.

Assets pass $500,000,000.

1936 January 22, Vice President Bertrand J. Perry elected president.

186

1937 January 1, adoption of "documentary form" of policy.

Company begins to insure sub-standard risks.

1938 Policies in connection with Pension Trust plans first issued.

1939 First agents' Home Office Training School held.

1941 Insurance first issued without medical examination.

1945 January 24, Bertrand J. Perry, president 1936-1945, elected chairman of the board of directors and Vice President Alexander T. Maclean elected president.

July 1, Career Contract adopted providing revised method of compensating agents and establishing contributory pension plan.

Assets pass one billion dollars.

1946 First Group policy issued.

Maximum age at issue increased from 65 to 70 years.

1947 October 16, adoption of Commissioners' Standard Ordinary Mortality Table and 2½% interest as the basis for premium rates and reserves.

1948 January 1, adoption of Massachusetts Mutual Employee Contributory Pension Plan.

June 30, after fifty-one years of service to the Company, Chairman of the Board Bertrand J. Perry retires from office but continues to serve on the board of directors.

First Renewable and Convertible Term policy issued.

Company begins insuring children one day old and over with full benefit at age one.

1949 Group Insurance for Home Office and Field personnel transferred from other carriers to Company's Group Department.

Company introduces "Design for Security," its unique programming plan for analysing individual's insurance and retirement needs.

1950 Adoption of new Disability clause, providing waiver of premiums and monthly income of $10 per month per $1000 of sum insured, with payment of sum insured as endowment at age 65 or upon prior death or maturity.

Insurance in force passes three billion dollars.

May 15, death of Alexander T. Maclean, president 1945-1950.

May 19, Vice President Leland J. Kalmbach elected president.

Extensive additions made to Home Office building.

1951 Home Office staff numbers 1350.

May 15, Massachusetts Mutual completes its first century of service.

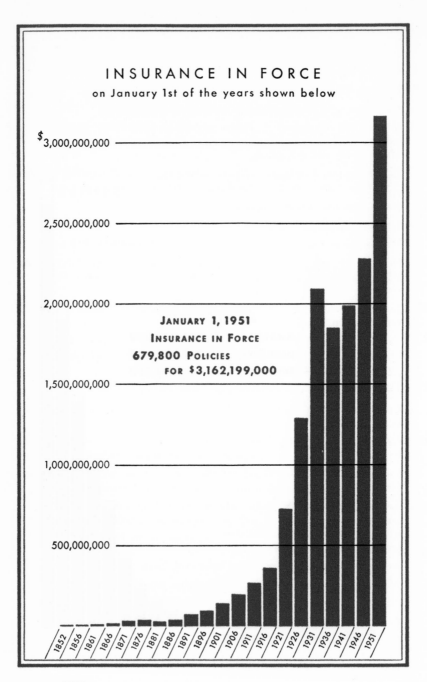

INSURANCE IN FORCE
on January 1st of the years shown below

$3,000,000,000

2,500,000,000

2,000,000,000

JANUARY 1, 1951
INSURANCE IN FORCE
679,800 POLICIES
FOR $3,162,199,000

1,500,000,000

1,000,000,000

500,000,000

1852 1856 1861 1866 1871 1876 1881 1886 1891 1896 1901 1906 1911 1916 1921 1926 1931 1936 1941 1946 1951

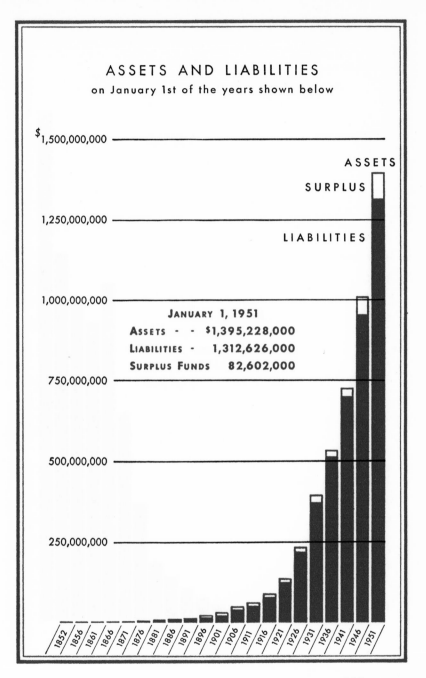

ASSETS AND LIABILITIES
on January 1st of the years shown below

$1,500,000,000 ————————————————————————

ASSETS

SURPLUS

1,250,000,000 ————————————————————————

LIABILITIES

1,000,000,000 ————————————————————————

JANUARY 1, 1951
ASSETS - - $1,395,228,000
LIABILITIES - 1,312,626,000
SURPLUS FUNDS 82,602,000

750,000,000 ————————————————————————

500,000,000 ————————————————————————

250,000,000 ————————————————————————

1852 1856 1861 1866 1871 1876 1881 1886 1891 1896 1901 1906 1911 1916 1921 1926 1931 1936 1941 1946 1951

EXHIBIT OF COMPANY'S PROGRESS

Record as of January 1,
the beginning of the following anniversary years:

	1876 JANUARY 1 TWENTY-FIFTH ANNIVERSARY YEAR	1901 JANUARY 1 FIFTIETH ANNIVERSARY YEAR
New Insurance Delivered (in the preceding calendar year)	$ 5,186,000	$ 22,353,000
Insurance in Force	35,029,000	136,238,000
Assets	6,102,000	26,245,000
Liabilities	5,537,000	23,921,000
Surplus Funds	565,000	2,324,000

	1926 JANUARY 1 SEVENTY-FIFTH ANNIVERSARY YEAR	1951 JANUARY 1 ONE HUNDREDTH ANNIVERSARY YEAR
New Insurance Delivered (in the preceding calendar year)	$ 205,729,000	$ 347,867,000
Insurance in Force	1,286,309,000	3,162,199,000
Assets	230,502,000	1,395,228,000
Liabilities	215,470,000	1,312,626,000
Surplus Funds	15,032,000	82,602,000*

*Includes Security Fluctuation Fund $10,000,000.

PAYMENTS MADE
BY THE MASSACHUSETTS MUTUAL
TO POLICYHOLDERS AND BENEFICIARIES
from organization in 1851 to January 1, 1951

	1851 TO **1951**
Payments to Living Policyholders	
Dividends to Policyholders	$ 374,400,000
Cash Surrender Values	304,700,000
Matured Endowments	107,900,000
Annuity Benefits	87,700,000
Disability Benefits	38,200,000
TOTAL PAYMENTS TO LIVING POLICYHOLDERS . .	$ 912,900,000

Payments to Beneficiaries	
Death Benefits	$ 569,600,000
Accidental Death Benefits	2,300,000
TOTAL PAYMENTS TO BENEFICIARIES	$ 571,900,000
GRAND TOTAL	$1,484,800,000

191

The pencil drawings illustrating this book are the work of Ray J. Holden of North Sterling, Connecticut. They, as well as the photographic illustrations, are reproduced in gravure by the Beck Engraving Company of Philadelphia, Pennsylvania.

The design of the book, the typography, letterpress printing and binding are the work of Schneidereith & Sons, Baltimore, Maryland.

The type is 12 point Linotype Baskerville.

The paper is Strathmore Book, Wove.